A

DEATH IN

THE SÁNCHEZ

FAMILY

A
DEATH IN
THE SÁNCHEZ
FAMILY

OSCAR LEWIS

Vintage Books

A DIVISION OF RANDOM HOUSE

NEW YORK

ACKNOWLEDGMENTS

I am most grateful to my wife, Ruth M. Lewis, for her assistance in the organization and editing of my original interviews with the children of Sánchez which form the basis of this volume. I am also grateful to Asa Zatz for his excellent translation from the Spanish; to Mrs. Allean Hale for editorial suggestions on an early version of the manuscript, and to Mr. Gordon Ray for helpful comments on the final manuscript. Finally, I want to thank Manuel, Consuelo and Roberto Sánchez for their cooperation in this study.

O. L.

Contents

Introduction

THIRTEEN years have passed since 1956 when I began my study of Jesús Sánchez and his children, Manuel, Roberto, Consuelo, and Marta, in a Mexico City slum. The publication of my book *The Children of Sánchez* in 1961 did not mark the end of the study nor did it terminate my relationship with the family. Indeed, we have been in constant touch and not a year has passed without my visiting them. Many important changes have occurred in their lives. However, in this book I shall limit myself to relating a single dramatic incident, the death of Guadalupe, the maternal aunt and the closest blood relative of the Sánchez children.

Although Guadalupe was only a minor character in my book, she played a central role in the Sánchez family. Moreover, she, her husbands, and her neighbors in the *vecindad* were better representatives of the way of life which I have called the culture of poverty than were Jesús Sánchez and his children, who were more influenced by Mexican middle-class values and aspirations. In December, 1962, one month after Guadalupe's death, I returned to Mexico to study the effects of her death upon the family. This book, based upon my tape-recorded interviews with Manuel, Roberto, and Consuelo Sánchez, presents three views of their aunt's death, wake, and burial.*

These three stories reveal the difficulties encountered by the poor in disposing of their dead. For the poor, death is almost as great a hardship as life itself. The Danish novelist Martin Andersen Nexö, writing in his autobiography about his early life in a Copenhagen slum, recalls that when he was about three years old he asked his mother whether his brother, who had recently died, was now an angel. His mother replied, "Poor people don't belong in heaven, they have to be thankful if they can get into the earth." The struggle to get Aunt Guadalupe decently into the earth is one of the themes of this book. A larger theme is how her death illuminated her life and how both her life and death reflected the culture of poverty in which she lived.

Guadalupe died as she had lived, without medical care, in unrelieved pain, in hunger, worrying about how to pay the rent or raise money for the bus fare for a trip to the hospital, working up to the last day of her life at the various pathetic jobs she had to take to keep going, leaving nothing of value but a few old religious objects and the tiny rented space she had occupied.

Guadalupe's entire life was one of deprivation and trauma. Born into a poor family in León, Guanajuato, in 1900, she was ten years old when the Mexican Revolution

---

* The youngest daughter, Marta, was not in Mexico City and did not attend the funeral.

began and was twenty when it ended. Thus she lived through some of the most difficult years in the history of Mexico, when bloodshed, violence, hunger, and much suffering occurred. Her sad experiences, not unusual for those times, help us to understand her situation at the time of her death.

Guadalupe was one of eighteen children, only seven of whom survived their first year. Her parents were religious and had been properly married in church. They were illiterate and earned a living by making sweets which they sold in the plaza. The extended family was small and they had few relatives to help them. Both sets of grandparents were dead by the time Guadalupe was born. She did not know where they originated but they were probably part of the urban proletariat in León. Guadalupe's parents spoke no Indian tongue and, as far as we know, they followed no tradition other than Mexican folk Catholicism. Of her family, Guadalupe said:

"The only relatives I knew were my *papá's* sister Juana and my *mamá's* sister Catarina. They lived a few blocks away. My Aunt Catarina was married to Juana's son, who was my *papá's* nephew. He was a porter who carried heavy loads on his back. He was tall and strong but the work finally killed him."

Guadalupe's parents spent a good part of the day working away from home. They arose at three o'clock in the morning to buy fresh bread which they sold in the plaza until noon, when they returned home to rest. At half-past four in the afternoon they left again to sell their sweets, often not getting home until two o'clock in the morning.

From about age five, Guadalupe, the eldest daughter, was left in charge of the house and of her younger brothers and sisters. The parents required all the children to rise at three in the morning to haul water for the garden before attending Mass at four. The boys spent the morning making sweets—squash and *camotes* baked with brown sugar and honey—and Guadalupe did the marketing, cooking, and other household chores. She had never been allowed to go to school or to play with other children and she recalled her childhood with a sense of martyrdom.

"My *papá* was very strict and wouldn't let us accept anything from anybody, even from relatives. Never. Once I remember we were crying with hunger and my Aunt Juana gave us some beans and *tortillas* and my *papá* came home with his tray of sweets and said, 'Who gave you that?' and I had to give back the *tacos*. He was angry and made my aunt cry.

"*Papá* was a very bitter man. He didn't allow visitors. The only ones who came to our house were the peddlers who bought boxes of sweets. *Papá* kept us locked in so that we wouldn't go walking around and entering people's houses. My brothers would fly their kites on the roof or they would run in the yard. I didn't play with them because they hit me. *Papá* was very careful with us. We never went to a movie or theatre or anywhere. He didn't like us to have friends and my sister and I weren't allowed to play with dishes or with dolls because he said with dolls we'd learn bad things.

"My life was very sad. My clothes were made from little pieces of scrap cloth, and we used felt slippers instead of shoes. I wore a long skirt and a blouse with long sleeves. Even though they had as many colors as a bird, with a patch here and a patch there, I was very happy when my *mamá* made me a new skirt. We never heard music in our house, nor did we dance. As for *fiestas* or the Christmas *posadas*, we only watched them from the roof. That was one of my greatest pleasures. And it wasn't until we came to Mexico City that we learned about receiving gifts on the Day of the Kings.

"When I went to the market I carried my youngest brother in my arms and the next-to-the-youngest (the jealous one) on my back and I held the basket in my hand. One day I was coming from the market and the police grabbed me because I wasn't in school. They said they were going to lock me up and I cried and cried until my *mamá* came. She and *papá* didn't send me to school because I was the only girl who could help at home. That's why I am no better than a donkey, because I can't read.

"My sainted mother didn't teach me anything but I learned to cook and wash all by myself. If the beans weren't ready at eleven when they came home to eat, my *mamá* would hit me. If I broke a dish she would scrape my hands with the pieces so I would be more careful. I was more afraid of her than of my *papá*. He was more affectionate and didn't hit me as often as she did. I was his favorite, but he beat me several times with a wet whip. Just to hear him speak made me tremble. When he and my *mamá* quarreled my *papá* would say, 'Those who want to come with me, come and those who want to stay, stay.' My older brother and I would always go with *papá* and *mamá* would get very angry. We would go out to the country for about a week selling Judas figures and sweets, and sleeping on the ground. When we went home again *mamá* would give us a long sermon.

"I began washing my *papá's* clothes when I was four. I was so little my hands couldn't hold the big pieces. I'd wash first one leg of his pants, then the other. When I was six, he bought me a little *metate* and a jar of corn dough and I made his *tortillas*. We didn't iron the clothes but by the time I was eight I could smooth them out and fold them."

At eleven or twelve, Guadalupe's menstruation came as a great shock, primarily because she was afraid of being punished by her parents. She hid all day in a deep hole in the hope that the bleeding would stop. When her mother learned of it she said to her daughter, "Don't be frightened, it happens to everyone."

"To rich people, too?" Guadalupe asked.

When Guadalupe was thirteen, Fidencio, a man of thirty-two, broke into the house when her parents were away and carried her off at knife point. He lived on the other side of the street and had made advances to her ever since she was nine. He took her to a cave and raped her. She bled profusely and he brought her to his mother's house in Hidalgo. Guadalupe stayed in bed unattended for fifteen days until the hemorrhaging stopped. Her father found her and whipped her so badly she had to be in bed another two weeks. He told her he didn't like girls who were deflowered because they weren't "worth anything anymore," and he forced her to marry Fidencio in church.

Guadalupe's mother-in-law disliked the girl and forced her to grind six *cuartillos* of corn every day and make large piles of *tortillas* to sell in the plaza. Guadalupe was often beaten by her husband and he took her from one aunt to another because his mother refused to keep her. Guadalupe did not realize that she was pregnant until she was about to give birth. She thought that somehow an animal had gotten into her abdomen and that she was going to die, but she said nothing about it. Fidencio was a soldier in the revolutionary army and when he realized her condition, he got an army pass and took her back to his mother. Guadalupe was about fourteen when she gave birth to her son Luis.

Guadalupe's mother-in-law continued to mistreat her. She kept her half-starved, giving her only wild greens without salt. When word came that Fidencio had been killed, Guadalupe was told she had to go back to Guana-juato. Her brother-in-law, a teamster who carried loads of beans and corn to Guanajuato, refused to take her with him although the countryside was full of roving brigands. She had to walk all the way, carrying her child in her arms. It was the rainy season and Guadalupe could find no food for herself and the baby. They almost died of hunger and they would have drowned trying to cross a flooded river, but a teamster saved them by pulling out Guadalupe by her braids.

In Guanajuato, Guadalupe learned that her elder brother had been killed while defending a friend and that her father had died of anger and grief. Her mother had gone with the children to Mexico City to stay with her Aunt Catarina. Guadalupe and a friend whose husband had also been killed in the revolution went after them, begging food along the way and often eating only banana peels or the shells of prickly pears. When Guadalupe arrived, her mother didn't recognize her at first and cried to see her daughter so emaciated and ragged.

Guadalupe's mother and her five brothers and sisters, as well as Guadalupe and her child, all lived with Aunt Catarina and her children in a one-room apartment in a poor section of the city called *colonia* Morelos. It was a crowded working-class neighborhood with many shops, markets, a few small factories and warehouses, public baths, third-class movie theatres, run-down schools, sa-loons, and *pulquerías* or taverns where native *pulque* was sold. There were few restaurants but many sidewalk kitchens that sold cooked food at low prices.

Guadalupe, her mother, and her sister Lenore sup-ported themselves by selling cake and spiked coffee at a little stand on a street corner. Of her four brothers, two worked in a bakery, one in a *pulquería*, and one was soon to die of typhus. Guadalupe, too, had typhus but she recovered and continued to work at the coffee stand. Putting alcohol in the coffee was a legal offense and Guadalupe went to jail three times either because her mother couldn't pay the fine or because her mother's new husband wouldn't let her. Fearful of being sent to the penitentiary if she were arrested once more, Guadalupe, who was nineteen by then, looked for another job. She went with a friend of the same age and before long the two girls were tricked into going to a brothel. Guadalupe was impressed by the fine beds she saw there because she had slept on straw mats all her life. An old lady told them it was a bad place and chased them out, but Guadalupe said, "How can it be bad if it has so many beds?" It wasn't until later that she understood what kind of a place it was.

After that, Guadalupe found a job as a chambermaid in a hotel, where she earned one *peso* a day.

When her son was five years old, Guadalupe's ex-mother-in-law, who was now living in Mexico City, asked to borrow him for a short time to see if he would help distract her remaining son from drinking. Guadalupe was having a hard time feeding the boy and she was afraid of her mother-in-law, so she agreed. She visited him every two weeks, bringing cake or fruit and a few *pesos* each time. However, her mother-in-law turned the boy against her and he would slam the door in his mother's face, sending her home crying. Finally, upon her brother's advice, she stopped visiting her son and he remained with her mother-in-law. Like his uncle, he became an alcoholic. Years later he died in a drunken binge.

Guadalupe learned from her mother-in-law that her deceased husband had been chopped up with *machetes* and dumped into a river. She had never loved him but she prayed for his soul and vowed to the Virgin of Guadalupe that she would never remarry because she had suffered so much as a wife.

Guadalupe then fell in love with Alfredo, who left his wife and child to go off with her. He became a lieutenant in the revolutionary army and she followed him to Matamoros, where he was stationed.

"With that man I had everything I needed. He dressed me well; I wore high-heeled shoes and only my toes touched the ground when I walked. He gave me fifteen *pesos* a day for expenses, but when my *mamá* wrote to me that she was starving while I was eating he let me go to work just so I could send her money. I killed myself working. I got up at three o'clock in the morning to go to the mill and I made *tortillas* and cooked for twenty-two soldiers. I washed and ironed for General Amaro because he liked my work and paid me twenty-five *pesos* just for a uniform. There were times I sent my *mamá* money orders for thirty or thirty-five *pesos*.

"Alfredo was good to me but he was very jealous. He didn't allow me to raise my eyes or leave the door open, but he chased after other women all the time."

Guadalupe was jealous, too, and Alfredo beat her for spying on him. When she became pregnant, he abandoned her. To keep from starving, she continued to take in laundry.

"I'd go to the river with my big belly, carrying a load of laundry on my head and I washed for the soldiers all day, half submerged in the water. What a life I led. All I ate were *tortillas* made of white flour, fried onions, and a can of condensed milk.

"I had a picture of Alfredo in his uniform and I would kneel before it as if he were a saint, crying and praying to hear from him again. 'Speak to me, Alfredo . . . just say one word.' My girl friend said he had bewitched my brain with a dark spirit and she took me to a Spiritist who cured me. I burned Alfredo's picture and didn't cry for him any more. I had loved him but he paid me back badly. After that I didn't believe in anybody."

She gave birth to her son Salvador in the camp and had a hard struggle to support herself and the baby. But she loved the child and did not complain. "God forgive me, but I never loved the first baby the way I loved little Salvador."

She followed the army, cooking beans and making *tortillas* for the troops during the day and barricading her door every night to keep out the soldiers. When they were disbanded, she and her son went to Veracruz, where she had been offered a good job as a maid. When she arrived the *señora* told her there was no money to pay her. Guadalupe worked without pay for three months, then fell ill with malaria. Swollen and shaking with chills, she went back to Mexico City on a military train.

When Guadalupe arrived she found that her mother and two brothers were no longer living with Aunt Catarina. She had forced them to move by awakening them at four o'clock every morning and making them wait outside in the cold while she washed the floor. Finally they moved into a little room of their own for which they paid only four *pesos* a month rent in exchange for janitorial services. The roof was only half covered and whenever it rained they would all get wet, but Guadalupe had no choice and moved in with them.

Guadalupe was ill with malaria for seven months without being able to find a cure. Her brother treated her with a mixture of sugar cane, *jicama* roots and water but it made her worse because they were "cold" foods. Her mother kept her in the sun and gave her a quart of green alcohol to drink with strong coffee; then they tried *pulque* with ground *pirú*; they put a mouse on her neck and they beat her brother in her presence to frighten her, but she didn't get better. Ashamed to eat without working, she went out to beg for food. One day a woman in the street took pity on her and cured her with *nopal* leaves, chile, and honey. By that time, however, because most of the remedies had contained alcohol, Guadalupe had acquired a taste for drinking.

When Guadalupe found a job making *tortillas* in a *tortillería* at $1.80 a day, she and her family moved to her brother Pedro's room on the Street of the Painters, where he was living with his common-law wife. Guadalupe stayed there for some time, then moved in with Lenore and Jesús Sánchez, her new brother-in-law. While Guadalupe had been away, Lenore had had an affair with a railroad worker who abandoned her and left her with a baby. Lenore found a job as a dishwasher in the La Gloria restaurant, where she met Jesús Sánchez and became his common-law wife.

Guadalupe had always believed that her mother favored her younger sister Lenore and was jealous of her.

"I worked to support my little mother, but she was very hard on me, may she rest in peace! My little son and I would cry because she didn't bring our lunch to the *tortillería*. She would forget all about us, but she never failed to bring a *taco* to Lenore. I asked my Aunt Catarina, 'Ay, Auntie, am I not my mother's daughter? Why does she love only Lenore?' My aunt would say that I had bad luck and that I must resign myself to it."

Guadalupe was about thirty years old when she met

Ignacio. He was twenty. He sold newspapers and every day he passed by the *tortillería* where Guadalupe worked. They became sweethearts and a year later began to live together as man and wife. However, because of her vow, Guadalupe refused to marry Ignacio.

Ignacio was living with his father and sister in a room at No. 6 on the Street of the Painters, where he brought Guadalupe and little Salvador. Later they moved to a room of their own at No. 30 on the same street. They had only a straw mat to sleep on, two blankets, and a soap box to hold their clothing, but they were happy and didn't complain. Guadalupe took in laundry and raised a few chickens and doves to help support her son. Ignacio worked from early morning to late at night to earn a few *pesos* selling newspapers. Salvador refused to go to school or become a carpenter's assistant as his mother wanted him to. Most of the time he played in the street while both parents worked. However, occasionally he helped Ignacio sell newspapers.

Guadalupe and Ignacio developed the habit of drinking *pulque* every night. As Salvador grew into his early teens he, too, began to drink. He was a quarrelsome, aggressive youth and was generally disliked. When Guadalupe and Ignacio were forced to move because their *vecindad* was being torn down, they had no one to turn to but Prudencia, the second wife of Guadalupe's brother Alfredo. Prudencia agreed to take in Guadalupe and Ignacio but she balked at Salvador. Salvador moved in with his parents anyway, bringing down upon them Prudencia's anger and abuse. She tried to force them to leave by locking them out, even when it was raining, but they had no place to move to and they would meekly stand huddled under newspapers until she relented and let them in.

Salvador took a common-law wife, with whom he had

a son, but she ran off with another man, taking the child. Salvador drank more than ever and one day, caught alone and drunk in the street, his wife's lover stabbed him to death with an ice pick. Salvador was twenty-four when he died. Prudencia refused to allow the coffin in her house, so it was placed in the courtyard and the wake was held outdoors. Years later when Prudencia's son went to an insane asylum, Guadalupe said, "Yes, we pay for everything we do in life. God is slow but he doesn't forget."

Ignacio and Guadalupe moved to the Panaderos *vecindad*, where for fourteen *pesos* a month they rented apartment No. 1. It was a large room and the only one with a window. The *vecindad* itself had a fence and a front door and was in better condition than at the time of our study. When the fence broke down, the landlord had it removed, leaving the *vecindad* completely exposed to the street. He did not replace it until 1962.

Guadalupe's mother and two brothers were unhappy living with Pedro and his wife and they moved in with Guadalupe and Ignacio. Guadalupe's brother Lucio soon took a neighbor, Julia, as his common-law wife. They lived together for only a short time because Lucio died of drink. Not long thereafter, Guadalupe's mother died of cancer and her other brother left.

With the exception of the one brother who died of typhus, all of Guadalupe's brothers died of drink. Even her father was drunk when he died. Guadalupe and her sister Lenore also drank. Her mother was the only one in the family who abstained. Lenore suffered from liver trouble and other conditions which were aggravated by alcohol. Her sudden death at twenty-eight, when she was pregnant with Jesús' fifth child, may also be partially attributed to drink.

Guadalupe took care of her dead sister's children until

her brother-in-law, Jesús, found another wife. He had made advances to Guadalupe and at one time suggested that they live as man and wife to keep the family together, but she had refused.

"If I had been different, I would have accepted. Jesús was strict and serious and liked to have other women but he was a good provider. With Ignacio I suffered the blackest pain because when it rained, he couldn't sell his newspapers and we didn't eat. Then, for two years he left me for another woman and came back sick and dirty and full of lice. He had seven women besides me but I was the only one who could stand him. Jesús might have won out but after having been with Ignacio so many years, how could I accept?"

Guadalupe and Ignacio continued to live in the Panaderos *vecindad*, although the landlord divided their large room in two and rented the front part, containing the window, to a shoemaker. The remainder, still called No. 1, was a small dark room with a tiny anteroom for a kitchen. In the nine years they lived here, they managed to furnish it with a narrow iron bedstead and spring, but no mattress, an old wardrobe, a small wooden table, a shelf for an altar, a large chair, and two small stools. All of these were bought second-hand. There was a blanket, a pillow, and a sheet for the bed, a second-hand charcoal brazier for cooking, a few clay pots, jars, cups, glasses, and plates and spoons but no table knives or forks, no clock, and no radio at the time of our study. Guadalupe's collection of religious pictures, some hanging in frames, others tacked to the wall, was the largest in the *vecindad* and a source of great pride to her. Two of the pictures had been passed down from her grandmother and she considered them heirlooms.

In this humble home the Sánchez children had sought

temporary refuge at various critical points in their lives; Manuel at fifteen when he decided to live in free union with his first wife, Paula, Roberto when he was released from jail and again when he needed a home for his first woman, Consuelo when she left her father's home in a fit of jealous rage toward her young stepmother and again when she was out of work, and Marta who came with her three small children when she was abandoned by her first husband. Guadalupe and Ignacio were always ready to share their little floor space and whatever food they had.

The Panaderos *vecindad*, where Guadalupe lived, consisted of a row of fourteen one-room adobe huts built along the left side and across the back of a thirty-foot wide bare lot. The lot was enclosed on two sides by the walls of adjacent brick buildings and in front by a recently built brick wall with a narrow open entrance that led to the courtyard. The only pavement in the yard was a walk of rough stone slabs laid by the tenants themselves, in front of the apartments. Five of the dwellings had makeshift sheds, constructed by setting up two poles and extending the kitchen roofs of tarpaper, tin, and corrugated metal over the low front doorway. The sheds were built to provide a dry, shady place for the artisans who lived and worked there. Piles of equipment, tin, bundles of waste steel strips, wire, nails, and tools kept on old tables and benches cluttered the covered space. Toward the rear of the yard, two large cement water troughs, each with a faucet, were the sole source of water for the eighty-four inhabitants. Here the women washed their dishes and laundry and bathed their children. In the back of the lot two broken-down stinking toilets, half curtained by pieces of torn burlap and flushed by pails of water, served all the tenants.

The rest of the lot, strewn with stones and filled with unexpected holes, was crisscrossed by clotheslines held up by forked poles. In the daytime, the lot was filled with children in ragged clothing and ill-fitting shoes, or barefoot, playing marbles or running between the lines of laundry, heedless of the warning shouts of the women. Children barely able to walk and still untrained, sat and crawled in the dirt, often half-naked, while their mothers watched them from where they were working. In the rainy season the yard became muddy and so full of water that it sometimes flooded the low dwellings.

The Panaderos *vecindad* was poorer and much inferior in every respect to the Casa Grande, where the children of Sánchez lived. Panaderos had no paved courtyard, no garden or trees, no gate at the entrance, and no patron saint to guard it. The families in Panaderos had practically none of the luxury items of those in the Casa Grande. As one moved from the Casa Grande to Panaderos one found fewer beds per person and more people who slept on the floor; cooking was done with kerosene or charcoal rather than with gas, people ate only one or two meals a day and used *tortillas* and spoons rather than knives and forks, *pulque* was preferred to beer, and more clothing and furniture was bought second-hand rather than new. To go from Casa Grande to Panaderos was to move back in time—from cement to adobe, from aluminum to clay pots, from antibiotics to herbal remedies, from doctors to native healers.

Of the twenty-five heads of families in the *vecindad*, only nine were born in Mexico City. The other sixteen came from towns and cities in the states of Morelos, Mexico, Hidalgo, Queretaro, Guanajuato, and Aguascalientes. The average length of residence in the capital was 26.2 years; the range was from twelve to forty-nine years.

Most of the original residents of the *vecindad* came in extended family groups or soon helped relatives to find apartments there. Because of the low fixed rent and other economic factors, the tenants did not move away without good reason. The average length of residence in the *vecindad* was about fifteen years.

The basic productive unit in the *vecindad* was the family, with the father, mother, and children all contributing to their support. Forty-six (57.7 percent) of the eighty-four inhabitants were working, either at full- or part-time occupations. There was an average of 3.3 workers per household. Male heads of households made up 24 percent of the total work force and because their earnings were small and irregular, with much of it being spent on drink, every one of the wives and all but one of the children over ten years of age, also worked. Women and children made up 76 percent of the work force.

The economic activities and technical skills of the adults were basically similar to those of their parents who migrated to the capital. The men were mostly unskilled or semi-skilled laborers, artisans or vendors; none were factory or industrial workers and with the exception of news vendors, none had joined labor unions or any other organized groups. There was a wide variety of occupations with great instability of employment. The heads of households and their parents had a total of 168 occupations, thirty-eight of which were distinct. The younger men had twice as many different occupations as their fathers, indicating an increase in occupational opportunities and perhaps, too, greater difficulty in earning a living with a single occupation.

There were, at the time of our study, twelve different occupations for men and women in the *vecindad* and most families worked in two, three, or four of them. The occupations were: street vendor (of towels, alcoholic beverages, cooked food, and candy), newspaper vendor, shoemaker, shining shoes, mechanics helper, tinsmith, toymaker, bicycle mechanic, leather worker, washer woman, making a lottery game, and shop clerk. Work was done at home in ten of the dwelling units. There were five artisans who produced articles in very limited quantities. For women, selling was considered the most desirable work; washing clothes, as Guadalupe did, was the least desirable. Yet the clotheslines were almost always hung with laundry and there was much competition for a place at the wash tubs.

The great poverty of the Panaderos *vecindad* was revealed by the low rentals, the crowding, the low per capita income, and the low value of the material possessions of the tenants. The rentals were from twenty to thirty *pesos*, or $1.60 to $2.40, per month.* Thirteen of the fourteen dwelling units had only one room. Most of the rooms were about ten feet in width and fifteen feet in length, providing only about one hundred and fifty square feet of floor space. The average number of occupants per unit was six. There were nine occupants in four of the units.

In addition to the eighty-four permanent residents, the *vecindad* had a transient population of as many as ten homeless friends and acquaintances of *vecindad* families. Mostly single unemployed men or abandoned women and children, the visitors were allowed to sleep on the floor of the main room or the kitchen and occasionally took meals with the family.

The monthly per capita income in the *vecindad* ranged from $3.60 to $26.24; the average was $8.40. Guadalupe and Ignacio were among the very poorest with a monthly

---

* The current rate of exchange was 12.50 Mexican *pesos* to one U.S. dollar.

per capita income, based on their combined work, of only $5.20. When Ignacio died and Guadalupe took in Gaspar as her companion, the household income became more irregular. Gaspar, a shoemaker, earned more than Ignacio but because he drank heavily he often did not work.

The low income of these people was related to their low educational level. Guadalupe had no schooling at all and was completely illiterate. Ignacio had one year of schooling during which he learned to pray, to say the alphabet, and do simple sums. Because of his occupation as a newsboy, he learned to read a good number of printed words. Gaspar had only two years of schooling.

The educational level of the other residents of the *vecindad* was also very low. The average number of years of school attendance was 2.1; only one tenant had five years of schooling. The children had no more education than the parents and the rate of illiteracy was high—40 percent. The highest rate of illiteracy was among the residents with rural background. However, 42 percent of the city-born were also illiterate.

The combined value of all the material possessions in all the households of the *vecindad* amounted to only $4,729.55. The average value per household was $337.78. The range was wide, however. Guadalupe, whose worldly possessions were valued at only $121.13, ranked next to the lowest in the *vecindad*. The family with the highest income had goods that were valued at $936.78, almost eight times more than Guadalupe. Twelve of the fourteen households owned less than $480 worth of material goods.*

The Panaderos *vecindad* was more cohesive and less

* For a detailed analysis of the material possessions in the *vecindad* see Appendix.

impersonal than the Casa Grande and functioned almost as a large extended family. Every family in the small *vecindad* is bound to one or more other families by ties of kinship, *compadrazgo* (ritual kinship), and long acquaintance or friendship. Similar close personal ties existed with individuals living in the neighborhood and *colonia*; ties farther away were fewer and weaker. Most of the *vecindad* residents spent the greater part of their lives within the narrow limits of the *vecindad* and its surrounding streets. Except for the ambulant vendors and those who occasionally go to public hospitals and religious shrines, these people make little use of other areas and are unacquainted with the city as a whole.

Kinship ties, either by blood or by marriage, linked thirteen of the fourteen dwelling units; related families tended to live next door to one another. Guadalupe was related to two families in the *vecindad*; Julia in No. 5 was her former sister-in-law and Matilde in No. 14 was the niece of Guadalupe's husband, Ignacio. One family had relatives in five separate units. There were eighteen types of consanguinal (blood) relatives and seven types of affinal (by marriage) relatives represented. Affinal ties were not as strong as blood ties and if a marriage dissolved, in-laws, step-parents, and step-children tended to be dropped.

Over half of the fifteen married couples in Panaderos lived together in free union. Both of Guadalupe's husbands in this *vecindad* lived with her in free union. However, her first husband in Guanajuato married her in church. Of the remaining half of the married couples in the *vecindad* approximately 30 percent were married by both civil and church law; two couples were married by church and by civil law alone. In five of the fifteen marriages, both spouses had lived in Panaderos before they were married; in eight cases one spouse, usually the wife, had lived there previously; only two older couples had come already married. The tendency toward endogamy or marrying within the *vecindad* was increasing among the younger generation.

The strongest ties were with maternal relatives. There were six matrifocal extended families whose members occupied all but one of the dwellings. Three families included four generations and twelve families included three generations. Eleven families had a grandmother living in the *vecindad*, and only one had a grandfather; four had a great-grandmother and none had a great-grandfather. In three households, a woman without a husband headed the family. Although married children were closer to their mother than to their father, the majority of young children in the *vecindad* had their father present in the home. Of the thirteen families with dependent children, the fathers in eleven of them lived at home. Nine of the families consisted of the father, the mother, and their children, with no other relatives present.

Relatives outside the *vecindad* were also very important, particularly those within the *colonia* Morelos. The families in the *vecindad* had a total of 1,245 relatives living in Mexico City. Of these, 369 (29.5 percent) lived in the same *colonia* and 876 (70.5 percent) lived elsewhere. The nearer relatives reside to one another, the stronger their ties, not only because it is easier and less expensive to visit, but also because they tend to be in the same socio-economic level. The more successful people move away from the slum and from the extended family.

Compadrinazgo, the system of ritual kinship which establishes a special respect relationship between the parents and godparents (*compadres*) of a child and between the godparents (*padrinos*) and godchildren (*ahijados*), was very strong in the *vecindad*. Of the fourteen dwelling

units, thirteen had ties of *compadrazgo*. There were
thirty-six children with *padrinos* in the *vecindad*. The
tenants generally chose *compadres* from among friends
rather than relatives, thus strengthening and formalizing
the friendship. Of the fifty *compadrazgo* relationships in
the *vecindad*, forty-seven were between unrelated families.

There were nine different types of *compadrazgo* in
Panaderos: baptism, confirmation, first communion, marriage, penance, blessing an image of the Christ child,
blessing a saint, *evangelios* (praying in church for a sick
child), and *medidas* (tying a blessed ribbon on a child to
protect him from disease). Confirmation was the most
frequent type of *compadrazgo* in the *vecindad*. Guadalupe had two *compadres* of penance, two of the Christ
child, and two of *medidas*. Two families had eight *compadres* in the *vecindad*; two others had seven *compadres*
and three had six *compadres*. Almost all of the tenants
had *compadres* outside of the *vecindad*, most of whom
were friends or former residents of the *vecindad* now living elsewhere in the same *colonia*.

The number and variety of *compadrazgo* relationships
in this little *vecindad* in the heart of the city was greater
than what had been reported for most Mexican rural
communities and provided an interesting reversal of the
usual trend toward secularization as one moves from the
country to the city. The proliferation of the *compadre*
system in the *vecindad* served as a stabilizing factor in an
otherwise loosely structured community and helped to
contain the tension and irritability which resulted from
the poverty, the crowded conditions, and the general lack
of privacy of *vecindad* life. The taboo against sexual relations among *compadres* was another stabilizing factor.

None of the residents of Panaderos *vecindad* came

from Indian villages, spoke an Indian language, or wore Indian clothing. Most of them had migrated to Mexico City from Guanajuato, where there was no Indian influence. Nevertheless, their religious beliefs and practices, although essentially of Hispanic tradition, represented a fusion of Indian and Spanish elements.

Central to the celebration of the Day of the Dead in the *vecindad* is the folk belief that the souls of the dead, first of children, then of adults, return to their families on November 1 and 2, respectively. This belief is especially strong among the poor, and as one moves up the economic and social ladder, the more formal Catholic beliefs begin to predominate. This is clearly seen in a comparison of the Panaderos *vecindad* of Guadalupe, with that of the Casa Grande of the Sánchez children. In Panaderos, 91 percent of the heads of families believed in the coming of the dead, whereas in the Casa Grande only 34 percent believed this. In neither *vecindad*, however, was there agreement as to the nature of the soul, how it returned, or when it arrived and departed.

In traditional Mexican villages, where there was a strong Indian element, five types of offerings were made for the returning soul on the Day of the Dead: a candle to light its way, water to quench its thirst, flowers to honor it, food to nourish it, and incense to guide it to its former home. In the Panaderos *vecindad* a much higher percentage of families followed this tradition than in the Casa Grande. Moreover, there seems to be a definite order in which these traits drop out as one moves up the social ladder. First to disappear is the incense, next, the food offering, and then the flowers. The offerings of candles and water were the most stable items and persisted the longest. In the Panaderos *vecindad*, only four families burned incense. Guadalupe, coming from a non-Indian area, did not burn incense but she followed the other rituals when she could afford them. On the last day of her life, which happened to be the Day of the Dead, she had left an offering of candles, water, and flowers for her dead relatives.

Guadalupe must have known that upon her death she would have no one to carry on the tradition for her. Neither Jesús Sánchez nor his children, her only relatives, celebrated the Day of the Dead as she did. Nor did they follow formal Catholic tradition of going to Mass, lighting a candle in the church, and placing flowers on the grave.

PART
I

The Death

Manuel

𝖨𝖳 was November 2, the Day of the Dead, and I was still in bed at about eleven-thirty in the morning when we heard someone knock. My wife opened the door to the courtyard and a voice outside said, "Good morning. Is *Señor* Manuel in?"

"Yes, he's here, but he isn't up yet."

"Who is it?" I shouted.

"Pancho, *Señor* Manuel." Pancho was the husband of my aunt's niece and right off I had a premonition of what he had come to tell me. "I just came to tell you that your Aunt Guadalupe is stretched out on the floor of her house, bleeding."

I sat up quickly, pulled on my trousers, and bent down to look under the bed for my shoes. I put them on without bothering to look for socks. Pancho said, "Well, I'm going now. Don't take long, *Señor* Manuel."

"All right, thank you," I called, "I'll be there right

away." I ran a comb through my hair and looked around for my jacket.

"Get going, Manuel, your aunt may be dead already, hurry up!" Maria said.

"All right, *hombre*, I'm coming. Go to the market and tell Roberto to fly to my aunt's house. Move, woman! Tell him to go right away, even if he hasn't sold anything yet."

As I started for the door, in walked Gaspar, that character my aunt took up with after her husband died. I didn't like Gaspar and I have to admit that I was still a little angry with my aunt for what she did. I didn't say anything to her when she married him because I always try to hide my emotions, but deep down my reaction was negative. I thought, Oh, what's life really all about? After having loved my uncle for such a long time the first thing you know here she is with a new love. And she was sixty while Gaspar was only thirty-five. What could he be after except a home at her expense? He had sly little eyes and I figured him for a bad character from the first time I saw him. He was short and skinny with a yellowish brown skin and the typical strawberry nose of an alcoholic. He never looked good but on this morning he looked ghastly. One could see the anxiety in his face. His lips were dry and his teeth clenched so hard his cheekbones stood out more than usual. He said, "Please, please, come quickly. She's just stretched out there, she's killed herself . . ."

"What do you mean, killed herself?"

He stood with his arms hanging at his sides, nervously opening and closing his fists. "Well, I don't know, she's just lying there."

"Come on, let's go." I rushed through the door, down

the courtyard, and out of the Casa Grande. The Street of the Bakers, where my aunt lived, was two blocks away. As I hurried along I had the same guilty thoughts I always have when something like this happens. Poor old woman! How is it possible that she could die all alone like this? She who was always surrounded by people? And me so slow about helping her out. A hundred *pesos* means nothing to me but what pleasure it would have given her, even if it went for alcohol or to help someone poorer than herself. It really made her happy to help others. I should have come to see her more often, if only for appearance's sake. But no, why should I if I didn't feel it? And every time it would have cost me money I didn't want to give. Why be a hypocrite? Me, the eternal hypocrite, used that to excuse myself!

From the corner I could see people gathered at the entrance of my aunt's *vecindad*. Most of them had come just to satisfy their morbid curiosity and I felt uneasy as we approached. Fortunately, the landlord had put up a brick wall to hide the row of miserable hovels from the street and we pushed open a path through the crowd and entered the muddy yard.

Gaspar went ahead but it had been a long time since I had been there so I stopped a moment to look around. There were a few women at the wash tubs toward the rear of the yard, scrubbing as usual, for most families took in laundry. The rickety buildings, lined up along one side and in the back of the lot, looked as though any strong wind would blow them down. The common toilets, the snarling dogs, the dirty kids . . . I never could understand how anyone could come out of such a place with a smile on his face because living there could mean only one thing, that his entire life was a failure. That's why I've tried to keep myself indifferent to the people there . . . because I had enough problems of my own. If they asked me for money and I didn't have it I'd feel like I was no good either. The whole place cried of poverty, of hunger, of every kind of need. It looked like a drawing by Posada, made sixty or seventy years ago. The only thing modern there was the hum of the motor in the carpentry shop at the left of the entrance. That and the TV aerial sticking up from the roof of Guillermo Gutiérrez's house.

A small crowd of people blocked the doorway of my aunt's house, which was the first in the row, next to the shoemaker's shop. Julia, the wife of Guillermo, saw me and said, "We've already called the ambulance, Manuel. She's dead." The crowd formed a circle around me, watching me closely. I said nothing and went quickly inside to see my aunt.

Yes, there she was, on the floor, with Gaspar sobbing over her. Her small body was curled awkwardly, her right cheek resting on the cold cement in a puddle of blood. Her right arm was caught beneath her, with only the palm of her hand showing; her left elbow pointed rigidly toward the ceiling. A sewing basket was clutched in her left hand. I could see the silver ring and the four copper ones she always wore on that hand. Her long dress covered her almost to the ankles. Her feet in their worn black shoes lay in another pool of blood. I bent over her to see if she was still breathing and I felt for her pulse, but there was nothing. The only thing that moved was her thin white hair, blowing in the cold draft that came in through the open doorway.

I looked at her face and its quiet sweetness comforted me a little. It was as if in the brief moment between life and death she had looked into the distance with the inner eyes of her soul and had seen a beautiful place, flowered and peaceful, where she would no longer suffer hunger and misery.

On the right wall of my aunt's poor little room, the holy images of saints and virgins in their wooden frames contemplated without grief the lifeless body on the floor. The picture of my dead mother on the rear wall seemed to stare at me reproachfully for having neglected her sister. Below the picture, between the bed and the wardrobe, was an unpainted pine table decorated with purple tissue paper and strewn with yellow zempazochitl flowers. On this my aunt had placed her offerings to her dead— several glasses of water and three cheap votive candles which were still burning. Being from Guanajuato, my aunt was "mocha," fanatically religious, and no matter what her financial state, she always provided something on the Day of the Dead. This year she hadn't had enough money to burn incense to attract the spirits of her deceased relatives or to buy fruit or chickens or bread for them, but she had left water so that the souls could at least quench their thirst, and candles to light their way. She even bought an extra candle for the dead who had no family to look out for them.

Flies were beginning to gather over the body and I brushed them away. I couldn't bear the scene any longer. Everything oozed of death. I went outside. There the children, trying to look in, were tearing at the cardboard patches on the outer wall of my aunt's kitchen. "What are you kids doing? Get out of here, go home!" I said. Some of the children moved away, but others took their places. The grownups boldly stretched their necks to look through the doorway.

"What happened? What happened?" people were asking everywhere, and others were telling what they knew. My irritation at their curiosity was rising.

"Well, didn't you hear, you blasted kids? Get going, take your noise elsewhere!" I said sternly, but no one paid any attention.

I went to ask Julia how it had happened. She was standing with Matilde, Pancho's wife, at the entrance of the *vecindad*, gabbing as usual. That woman always gave me the impression that her whole life passed through her lungs. Matilde, dressed as poorly as ever, had been the last one to talk to my aunt and was telling everyone about it. She repeated the story for me. Her face showed no sorrow as she spoke. She sounded as though she was telling about a movie.

"You see, Manuel, I came by this morning and said to Lupita, 'I'll bring you your *taquito* and coffee in a moment, auntie. How do you feel?' 'Fine,' she answered. Imagine! 'Ay, daughter, don't forget my little cup of coffee.' 'Now, aunt,' I said, 'didn't I say I'd bring it in a moment? And just think, I ground some chile sauce and meat in the mortar for you. You'll see, you're going to like it!' And I left. But before I got back, one of the kids came running up to my old man shouting 'Pancho, Pancho, Lupita is dead. She fell down and has a lot of blood coming out of her head.' So my old man comes out and sure enough, there she was on the floor. And right away he went to call you."

"Why doesn't the ambulance get here?" said Julia impatiently. "We've already called them three or four times and still those bastards don't come. And what about Roberto?"

"I've already sent for him, Julita, I don't think he'll be long." I stretched my neck toward the Street of the

Barbers, but neither the ambulance nor my brother was in sight.

"Ay, *hombre*, what a sad end for your poor aunt. And I can't even shed a fucking tear. I don't know why, I just can't," Julia said shrugging her shoulders, "but believe me, Manuel, God forgives people like her. At least her suffering is over, and she's rid of that ugly bastard Gaspar." None of the neighbors liked Gaspar because they thought he was taking advantage of my old aunt, and beating her, too.

When I had first heard that rumor I had gone to see her and to meet Gaspar face-to-face so he'd know she had someone to back her up. He was a shoemaker and it was risky because he could pull one of his knives on me. But both he and my aunt denied that he beat her. He said, "It's a bunch of lies from a bunch of jealous old women. Why would I want to do her harm if I love her? How much do I love you, old girl, how much? Tell him, tell *Señor* Manuel. Those women are just jealous of your marriage." While he was talking I was laughing inside and saying to myself, "You poor son of a bitch! How could anyone envy marrying a specimen like you?" He seemed like a simple kind of slob but my aunt always defended him and lost a lot of friends because of it.

"Tell me, Manuel," said Julia, "what are you going to do about burying her?"

"That's just what I was wondering. Here I've spent this whole month sick with the damned tonsillitis. I was just going to start working again, and now this. But, well, we'll do it somehow."

"Ay, *hombre*, we're screwed! Look at me, for instance. I'm still selling towels for my brother, but so what? I sell a hundred and twenty, a hundred and fifty, and only get my expenses. I don't have any capital to work with and there's no one to help me. No, man, we're really screwed."

I decided to wait by my aunt's door and I went back into the *vecindad*. Roberto arrived, pale and panting.

"Well, brother, what's up?"

"Go on in, but don't move her, because she's already dead."

"No!" That was all he could say, and he quickly went into the room. I followed, and there he was, caressing my aunt's white hair. He put his hand on her chest, hoping to feel her heart still beating. Then he started to lift her.

"No, little brother, don't move her. She's already dead. Can't you see she's lost all her blood?" And his eyes filled with tears.

"Poor thing . . . my poor dear aunt! *Ay*, Manuel, I feel so guilty. When I think how much money I've squandered that I could have given her. Just look at that," he said, pointing to the small charcoal brazier which showed no sign of having had a fire recently. "She hasn't cooked for days. And she always acted strong! Just the day before yesterday I asked her if she'd had lunch and she answered, 'Of course, meat and beans.' Meat and beans indeed! My poor little aunt. Now there she lies, the last of the Vélezes."

At this a great lump finally formed in my throat. "Yes," I said. "You're right. But her suffering is over now."

My brother looked as though he was about to cry. He was really upset. He felt closer to my aunt than I did and spoke affectionately of her but I had always thought it was just out of his own sentimentality because, sticking to the facts, my aunt never showed very much affection for him, or for any of us, in my opinion. My brother turned to her just to fill that tremendous feeling of emptiness and yearning for love that he has always had. That's why he was more loyal when it came to the family.

I never felt as if my Aunt Lupe was my mother because she never gave us that kind of love. I was fond of her because she was my mother's sister . . . a family tie, that's all it was. When my mother was alive, my aunt was a steady visitor at the house but that was because she enjoyed a little drink. My *mamá* was pretty active in that direction herself so that's why Lupita came around so often. But my mother was a go-getter and always had a *peso* or two more than my aunt and uncle did. So every time they came it was to have a meal or a drink or to borrow money.

When my mother died, my Aunt Lupita came to take care of us but she was there more as a servant because my father paid her a salary. She took care of us but I don't think it was anything more than a routine thing. The kind of obligation any person would have who was being paid to do it. She never went beyond that. It would never have occurred to her to give us a sign of affection or to say anything nice to us.

After that there was a period of years when I didn't see my aunt very much. If I went to her house (she was living with my Aunt Prudencia then), it was because her son Salvador was on a drunk or in a fight. Then, when I was fifteen, I put the choice up to Paula, the mother of my children, as to whether she'd live with me or go her own way. Aunt Lupita was the only relative of mine living nearby, so the most logical thing was for Paula and me to move in with her. My aunt didn't treat us so bad, or so good, either. She liked to be helpful to people and to have everybody think well of her but our relations were . . . well, I could see that she felt more affection toward the bums who came there to drink with her. She spoke to them with more confidence, as if she felt closer to them. With us, she used that tone of authority, just like my father. Sure it was gentler but it sounded pretty much the same to me. Born to command, just like my *papá!*

Our stay there ended miserably because my Uncle Ignacio wanted my wife to pay the rent with her body and I had to leave the place. I didn't see much of my aunt until after my uncle died. Naturally, when she felt she was getting old, she fell back on us. By then I was married to María and we would both go to see her. Each time it cost me five, ten, twenty *pesos,* but I must say Lupita never asked for a thing except when she was sick. We lived so estranged because maybe she was like me and wanted it that way. The farther away my family is, the less problems they cause me. In that way, I'm a little more independent. Maybe that's what she was trying to be, too.

"Listen," my brother said. "We've got to give her a decent burial. But how? Uncle Ignacio's funeral cost us five hundred *pesos.*"

"Well, we'll see about that, don't you worry."

"How can I help worrying? Look, I'll go see how much I can borrow from my godmother, though I owe her two hundred *pesos* already. If the ambulance comes don't let them take her away, because then it'll cost a lot of money to get her body out of there. I'll be right back."

He turned and left quickly. A little later we heard the ambulance siren screaming.

"Here they come, here they come!" chorused all the

neighbors and snoopers. The ambulance stopped at the entrance and a young doctor in a white uniform stepped out, with two stretcher bearers right behind him. I opened the rickety wooden door for him. He looked at the body and asked, "Well, what happened to this woman, *señor*? Just look at her!"

"I don't know, doctor, she was already like this when I arrived."

Gaspar stepped forward to give the doctor my aunt's card for the General Hospital. The doctor read the dates, shook his head, and said, "*Ay, qué caray*, there's nothing more we can do for this woman, she's dead. Now what you have to do is notify the police and they will certify the death. Meanwhile, don't move her."

"Then we shouldn't lift her?" I asked. Right away I realized what a stupid question it was. The doctor repeated, "No, don't move her. Take this card to the precinct to prove that this woman was being treated. Maybe they'll dispense with the autopsy."

The doctor and the bearers left and the crowd began to disperse.

"Well, Gaspar, go quickly to the police," I said almost in a tone of command.

"Yes, yes, *Señor* Manuel, I'll go right away. I won't take long."

Gaspar left and I took a stool and sat down outside the door. After I'd been sitting there a while a tall, thin, elderly woman came up to the door. Her eyes were sunken and her face so emaciated, she looked like death itself. She poked her head into the room and called "Lupita, Lupita . . ." Although she had seen me from the first, it wasn't until then that she spoke to me.

"Excuse me, but is *Señora* Lupe at home?"

"Yes, she's at home, *señora*. But she just died."

"What? Died! *Ay, ay,* Lord of Mercy, how can she be dead? I was with her only yesterday."

"Now, *señora*, calm down. Crying won't help matters." But she kept right on.

"Lupe was so good, the poor thing! She took me in when I didn't have a roof over my head. *Ay*, my God . . . Lord take pity on her, and forgive her all her sins."

Finally the woman calmed herself and sat down on the brick doorsill, pulling her skirt over her knobby knees and her ragged shawl over her head and long skinny arms. She began to move her lips silently, as if in prayer. And there we sat, she in her place and I in mine, each sunk in thought, without speaking or turning to look at each other.

Now that the public curiosity had been satisfied, we were finally left in peace. The neighbors were going about their regular tasks, kids running in and out of doorways, women coming and going with their shopping bags or kneeling at the wash tubs. The noise of the shoe shop in front of my aunt's house sounded louder than usual, and at the carpenter's across the yard, the saws screeched a gay hymn to life as they bit into the wood.

Señora Catarina, the news vendor's wife, came by and leaned into the doorway of my aunt's house to look at the body. Crossing herself and shaking her head from side to side, she started to leave. After a step or two, she turned back and said, "I'm going to market now, but as soon as I get back, if there's anything at all I can do . . ."

Then *Señora* Laura arrived. This woman had worked for a long time at the *pulquería* where my aunt and my deceased Uncle Ignacio used to buy their drinks.

"Excuse me, *señor*," she said, showing her big yellowed

teeth, "Is it true that Lupe is stretched out dead on the floor in there?"

"Yes, *señora*, unfortunately it is."

She kept pointing her finger at the floor inside the house and shaking her head, as if to deny it. After a while she said, "When I saw her yesterday she looked very bad to me. I said to her, 'Lupita, you'd better see a doctor,' and she said, 'Yes, Laura, I am. But there in the hospital they're just running me around. "Come back tomorrow, come back the day after tomorrow." And I keep coming back and coming back, but it always ends up the same way: "There aren't any beds, *señora*, come back tomorrow." ' So I told her, 'Yes, that's the way they are, the bastards, just because they see you're in bad shape. Well, don't go back any more. Let them shove their favors. Weak as you are, and all alone, something could happen to you out there on God's streets and then you'd be worse off than before. Let them go screw.' That made her smile a little, and she said, '*Ay*, Laura, you were always the one. Well, I have to be going. We'll have to knock off a *pulquito* when I have time. Right now I'm late.' And the poor old thing went off. She could barely walk. Yes, she was looking very bad already. My *compañera*, may she rest in peace."

Silence and remorse from me, and no comment. Laura continued, "Well, such is life. We can't call her 'poor thing' because God has already judged her. Poor us, who have to keep on struggling in this world."

At this point Gaspar came back from the police station, sweating from the walk. I got up quickly and asked, "What happened?"

"Nothing. The police don't have to come. All I have to do is go to the hospital and get the doctor who was treating her to give me a paper that says she is dead now."

"Then I guess we can lift her up off the floor."

The two women moved aside to let us into the room. As Gaspar knelt beside my aunt and put his arm under her neck, the tears began to pour from his eyes again. He laid his cheek against her white wrinkled one and began to speak to her.

"Little one, little one," he said, "you've gone and left me all alone now." The blood formed in threads on my poor aunt's face as Gaspar raised her head, and another phlegmy string dripped from her mouth to the floor. Squatting beside her, he put his other hand under her knees and tried to lift her by himself. A woman struggled to take off my aunt's shoes and one fell into the puddle of blood, splattering the woman's legs. Gaspar grunted in a useless effort to lift the body. I took my aunt by the wrists and together we lifted her to the bed. Gaspar sat down on the edge with my aunt on his lap and little by little slipped out from under her. The blood on her skirt stained his trousers red.

"*Ay*, look at that! Somebody clean her face!" one of the women said.

Gaspar took a rag, dampened it in the water pail, and began to sponge the matted gray hair. The blood remained stubbornly caught in the wrinkles of her skin.

Suddenly *Señora* Laura said, "Take a look and see if she didn't cut her head open."

With his big thick nails, all black underneath, Gaspar began to separate small strands of hair and to hunt between them. He stooped over and peered closely as his bloodied hands moved back and forth, over her head, searching and searching. Meanwhile, *Señora* Laura was cleaning up the blood on the floor.

I couldn't take it any more. I said to the women, "Please see if she has any clean clothes and change her. Would you please?" And, nearly throwing up, I left the room. I went over to the wash tubs to wash my hands. "Poor Laura," I thought, "she doesn't know that my aunt had cancer, and there she is, handling her blood. I'd better go to the house and bring back the alcohol for her to clean her hands with." I had just stepped out of the entrance when Gaspar called me. "Listen," he said, "I feel ashamed to mention it . . . but I have to go to the hospital to take care of the death certificate and . . . well, I don't have the bus fare."

"Oh, sure. It's good you reminded me. Please try to get it done right away."

He went off down the street and I continued on to my house, found the alcohol, and went back to my aunt's.

No one was there but the emaciated-looking woman who had arrived first. *Señora* Laura was gone. They had dressed my aunt and changed her position; now her feet were toward the door. I put the bottle of alcohol on the wardrobe and sat down on a little wooden bench.

"Say, young man, are you Lupe's nephew?"

"Yes, *señora*."

"And is the dark fellow your brother?"

"Yes, *señora*, my brother Roberto."

"*Ay*, young man, look, I want to tell you something. I don't want you to think that I'm interfering in things that are none of my business . . . but now that that devil Gaspar is gone, I would like you to know how he treated your aunt. I lived in Lupita's house so I know."

"Ah, yes. *Señora*, excuse me, what is your name?"

"Elvira, at God's service and yours. Well, he treated her very badly. That man has an evil heart. What was the use of his having lived with her? When her time came, wasn't she left all alone to die like a dog? Where was he? And another thing. He was always beating her, and he could hardly wait for her to get together a few *pesos* so he could take them away from her and get soused. One night when I was half asleep on the floor I heard a whack, whack, whack . . . I pulled myself up and I saw the damned fellow slapping Lupe right on the back of the neck. So I said to him, begging your pardon, 'Listen, you son of a so-and-so, why are you hitting her?'

" 'Is it any of your business, you old such-and-such?'

" 'Yes, it is my business. A man should support a woman, not beat her, you dirty no-good gigolo.' So then he got out of your aunt's bed and told me to go and do I-knew-what to my sainted mother, may she rest in peace. Only a couple of days ago, when you could see she was on her last legs, he said to her, 'You are going to leave everything in here to me, aren't you, *mamacita?*' Now I ask you, what kind of a thing to do is that? The poor thing wasn't even dead yet and this ape already had his claws out. For that reason alone my friend Lupita's things shouldn't go to him. He's a foul-mouthed bum, especially when he's drunk."

As she spoke I felt my blood getting hot but all I said was, "Don't worry, *señora*, we'll see about this."

At that moment Laura returned with a woman named Chita, who had also lived in my aunt's house. When Chita saw my aunt stretched out there, she burst into tears. She finally dried her eyes on the sleeve of her old sweater and said, "If that skunk Gaspar hadn't thrown me and my children out of here in the middle of the night I would probably have been with her at the last. But no, no . . . to die alone . . . all alone . . ." And she began to cry again. "Poor Lupe. I don't understand why she took so much from that miserable man. I used to see them fighting, but I couldn't interfere. You always end up the loser, with one person or the other. And anyway, after a fight they would get up the next day as if nothing had happened. Poor Lupe . . . very often she would sleep with me and the children on the floor because that son of a bitch was annoying her. She'd say to me, 'He can see how sick I am, yet he keeps bothering me. He has no consideration.' And then he would start, 'No, you rotten old bitch, you're no good for anything.' And he'd cut loose with things I don't believe even a porter in the market would say."

"Yes, he's very common," commented Elvira.

"You see," Chita continued, "that's why after a while nobody wanted to give Lupita a *taco* because she saved everything for her 'king' as she used to call him. Oh, he had it good, all right, that gentleman . . . the airs he put on! 'No son of a bitch has anything to say around here but me. This is my house and I give the orders.' His house, indeed! But what could I do? I was only taken in off the street."

I listened to the complaints, looking from one to the other. "So this fellow still kept on bothering my aunt?"

"Yes, man! She used to say, 'Damn it, Chita, my being old wouldn't matter so much if at least I was strong and healthy.' Whew, the way he used to insult the poor woman!"

Then my Aunt Prudencia arrived and joined our little group. She was the ex-mistress of my Uncle Alfredo, may he rest in peace. She, too, began to reminisce about the virtues of my departed aunt. She said that when my aunt worked in the restaurant, she used to bring Prudencia boxes of meat and bread and milk. "Yes, your Aunt Lupe helped me very much," Prudencia said. "That's why I told my sons that whoever had money in his pocket should stop by and give it to Aunt Lupe, now that she was in need."

After a while my stomach began to growl, reminding me that I hadn't had breakfast yet, and it was nearly four o'clock. I excused myself and went out into the courtyard to see if my brother was coming. *Señora* Laura followed me out.

"Listen, young man, why don't you go and see *Doña* Lila at the Barros Mortuary about the burial? She knew Lupe very well. Maybe she'll give us a low price."

"All right. I think we should go see her as soon as my brother comes back."

Finally Roberto arrived. "How did it go?" I asked.

"Not too well. I couldn't find my godmother, but I left word that she should come here."

"Good. You hang around here for a while and I'll see what I can do."

Señora Laura and I walked over to the undertaker's. A hearse was being washed at the curb. We went in and I spoke to the woman. Just as Laura had said, the cheapest funeral was five hundred *pesos*.

"All right, *señora*, I'll let you know in about an hour. Excuse me."

"Certainly. You saw that the casket is of good quality, padded and everything."

"Yes, *señora*, thank you very much." At that moment I had only twenty-five *pesos* in my pocket.

Señora Laura went back to my aunt's house and I went off to Gilberto's to have something to eat. At Gilberto's they were still celebrating his granddaughter's birthday party which had started the day before. I told them about my aunt but none of them, even in pretense, offered to accompany me at the wake. If I had been giving a party, they all would have come. What they say is true: the living get the chicken, the dead get the hole. Oh, well, that's life! After I ate I went to my house to lie down for a few minutes and my brother came in.

"Listen, Manuel, don't make any arrangements for the funeral; they've already brought the coffin and the candlesticks. My aunt has been laid out. Gaspar arranged everything."

"Well! And how much is it going to cost?"

"Four hundred *pesos*. Okay?"

"Well, at Barros' it was five hundred, so you saved a hundred."

My brother left, puffing at a cigarette, and I got up to heat some water to bathe my feet. When I was through, I put on my black leather jacket and went back to my dead aunt's house.

Roberto

WHEN my Aunt Guadalupe began to complain that she had a lump on her behind and that it bled and hurt a lot, I asked her, "Aren't you doing anything for it?" She replied, "Yes, of course, Gaspar is treating me." If it wasn't Gaspar it was another of those people she thought had magical powers.

There was a time when she wanted to go to the hospital to be cured but I couldn't take her right away because I was out of a job. "Give me a few days to find work, so I'll have money to take you to a private doctor," I told her. But when I saw that she was getting worse I said, "Look, aunt, if you want to go to the hospital, go ahead. You will be much better off. Everything is clean there, and at least you will get three meals a day. I don't believe that Gaspar takes care of you, even though you say he does. I'm sure you don't eat enough."

"Ay, no," she said, "but Gaspar is out of work. The

other day that good-for-nothing boss had him make some shoes and hasn't paid him yet. Can you imagine?"

"If Gaspar can't find work in one place he should look in another where they can pay him."

She always told me the same story, because that's what Gaspar told her. But I could see through him. He didn't know that I, Roberto Sánchez Vélez, was the King of the Liars. I never believed Gaspar's stories although it is true that he knew how to work. He would get his tools together, a knife, a hammer, some pliers, and would work well for a few days, but after a while he would pawn them so he could go get drunk. The result was that my aunt never had three meals in one day, I am sure of that. This hurt me very much, because I felt to blame for what had happened to her. When I had had money, more than enough to have given her some, I hadn't done it. Oh, I had helped her a little, but it wasn't enough. And this disgusted me very much. I said to myself, Well, what am I going to do? For a moment I was tempted to steal. I used to be able to get two, three, or four thousand *pesos* easily, but I was harming half the people in the world without realizing it. My only thought had been for what I could get for myself. But I honestly didn't want to do it anymore, because—it is no disgrace to say it—I don't know why, but before God I was afraid.

When I was working for General Electric I would give my aunt three or four *pesos* every day. I gave them to her gladly, with all my heart. But when the job at General Electric ended I couldn't give her even one *peso*. And so it went until the time came when I told her, "All right. I will come tomorrow to take you to the hospital." And she said, "I will appreciate it with all my heart."

The next morning I got five *pesos* together somehow

and came running over. My aunt wasn't ready. After greeting me she came out and said flatly that she wasn't going to the hospital because she was afraid of dying, afraid that they would experiment with her body and would disembowel her.

"Don't be foolish, auntie," I told her. "The science of medicine is very advanced and you needn't be afraid of dying. Besides, we all have to come to an end some day." I tried to cheer her up, but with her constant fear of death, she repeated, "Look. I absolutely am not going." I said, "All right, aunt, if you don't want to go, it's up to you." And I left. Actually, I felt a little relieved. I thought, "I'm not going to bother visiting her any more."

On the following day, there I was with her again. This time everyone in the *vecindad* told me how Gaspar had beaten her up, so again I spoke to her.

"Look, aunt. I don't want to interfere in your life, but wouldn't it be better to throw out Gaspar? He doesn't work; you even have to give him his clothes and his meals, big as he is. Let him get a young girl of eighteen or twenty to look after him. You're too old for him."

It was no use. My aunt defended Gaspar so I kept silent. I don't know if it was because of affection for him or for convenience, because once she told me, with great bitterness, "Well, what do you want me to do? I don't have a family any more, not even you people, because you don't help me. I have to stay with this man. At least he gives me beans to eat."

Many times I tried to insist that she move over to my house.

"No, son, I won't leave here until they carry me out, feet first." That's what she said, and that's how it turned out.

Then, about two weeks before my aunt died, my sister

Consuelo came here from Nuevo Laredo, where she had taken Manuel's children. She was trying to arrange for them to go to school across the border so she had to run all over the city getting the papers signed. Finally she got around to visiting my aunt.

"And how are you, little mother, so lovely, so precious . . ." She gave her a kiss, and the old woman greeted her with tears of pleasure. She was like that, always crying. So they kissed and hugged. When Consuelo found out my aunt was sick she immediately took charge and went with her to Dr. Ramón.

The next day my sister said to me, "Listen, Roberto, how barbarous you are, how inhuman, how useless!" She blamed me entirely for not taking care of our aunt. Why hadn't I taken her to a doctor, why hadn't I helped her, why this and why that?

She was probably right but I told her she shouldn't talk like that because I was doing more for my aunt than anyone else. "You! You haven't tried anything," she replied. She had Dr. Ramón's prescription filled and after several days went by she said, "This medicine is not doing any good. I think we are going to have to take her to Dr. Santoyo."

"*Caray*, sister, Santoyo charges twenty-five *pesos* for an office call and fifty if he comes to the house and I don't have any money right now."

"All right," she said, "but we have to take her to Dr. Santoyo."

"Look," I told her, "I have to go to the plaza to sell something because my wife and child must eat. I can get along on *tacos* filled with air, but they need food."

"Well then," she said, "here are the twenty-five *pesos* for the doctor."

"All right," I said. "I'll do it."

That day turned out to be a very bad one in the plaza. I didn't earn a cent and there was no food at home. We didn't even have milk for the baby and had to give him rice water with sugar. So I felt obliged that evening to use ten *pesos* from Consuelo's twenty-five for milk, bread, and rice. At night a neighbor of mine came over and I said to him, "I have a little problem. Could you lend me ten *pesos* until Saturday?"

"Yes, of course, *Señor* Roberto, here you are." So the next day I took my Aunt Guadalupe to Dr. Santoyo. We had to go by bus because there wasn't enough money for anything else. I said, "Look, old woman, forgive me, I know that the bus shakes you up, but do you think you can stand it?"

"Yes, yes, let's go, boy," she said, "as long as I get there." So we went. There were two or three patients ahead of us, and as there was a chapel in the clinic on the floor above I took my aunt upstairs and we both prayed a while together. It was nice there and my aunt felt better after asking her favors. Then we went back and waited for our turn.

"Who's next? Are you next?"

"Yes, Dr. Santoyo."

"Ah, very good, come in." We knew each other because he had taken out my appendix and had treated my wife. He said, "All right. What's the matter?"

"Well, Doctor," I replied, "I don't know exactly what my aunt's trouble is, but I brought her here for you to find out."

"Let's see, little woman, what's the matter? Tell me."

"Well, Doctor, it's that . . . no . . . I don't like to say it, but look, I have a big lump here on my tail, and it pains me a great deal, and it bleeds. *Ay, Dios mío,*" she had said, "I have to use a bunch of rags here inside. My husband, this Gaspar, is curing me, and the *Señora* Elvira is treating me too." She talked to him with as much confidence as if she had known him all her life.

"We'll see," said the doctor. "You wait outside."

I went outside. It took only about five minutes.

When she came out, she told me, "Look, he gave me this medicine, a salve." Actually, the salve was for hemorrhoids. I know because he prescribed the same thing for my wife. Dr. Santoyo, who was behind me, whispered, "Cancer." I could scarcely read the words on his lips. He said, "Tomorrow go to the General Hospital. You can find me in ward thirteen."

The next day Gaspar and my aunt went to the hospital alone. When they got there they were sent all over and told to come back the next day.

The next day I took my aunt back again. Gaspar came with us. All that happened was that a nurse wrote down information about my aunt's symptoms.

"*Ay*, that old nurse is mean," my aunt said. "She speaks roughly to me. 'Stand here,' she says, 'go over there. Don't shake so much.' It's like an ice box in there. I felt like a seltzer bottle that had been put into a refrigerator. My fingers were twisted with the cold. Would God have put us into the world and not expected us to shake when it was cold?"

Ay, Dios mío, I thought to myself, why do we have to put up with such misery? To my aunt I said, "Ah, it's the people who don't have any money who get this kind of treatment. But don't worry, if that nurse says anything tomorrow you can tell her where to go." I just wanted my aunt to know that I was backing her up all the time.

In the days that followed, Gaspar continued taking

my aunt to the hospital. And every day I would go by her house to see how she was and find out what they had told her.

They did nothing for her there at the hospital, absolutely nothing. They made her waste her time miserably and spend money that she didn't have. My aunt had advanced intestinal cancer, and it was incurable. Ramón, our family doctor, told me that my aunt would not get better even if San Martín de Porres, who is now so popular, would come down to her. "No," he said, "your aunt will not get well."

During this time my little boy got an infection from the milk, and there I was without any money. I had to run all over, pawning this and that. I pawned my windbreaker that I knew I wouldn't get back.

On November 1, All Souls Day, I had earned very little money, only six *pesos*, and I went to her house and saw everything so wretched, so pitiable, and—*ay*, it tears my heart when I remember this. How I wanted things to be different! My wife, my son and I at least had beans to eat, but the poverty of my aunt! I told her, "*Caray*, aunt, this was a very bad day for me. I made practically nothing. But look, I brought six *pesos*. Take two of them and I'll take the rest home to buy milk for the boy." I wasn't telling her the truth, because powdered milk costs fourteen *pesos* a can and I only had four left. Then she said, "*Ay*, son, don't worry about me. You might give it to your son and to Andrea." I told her they had plenty to eat so she accepted the two *pesos*.

"Good-bye, and God bless you, and Martincito de Porres, the Holy *Señor* of Chalma . . ." She always commended me to all the saints, and perhaps they have helped me more than once. I left in despair, saying to myself, She is going to die, I know it for sure. I don't think she'll last out the year.

On Saturday, the second of November, at about ten in the morning, I went to my brother's house. I had meant to go to my aunt's as I had promised, but I thought I should get at least a *peso* for her, so she could have some breakfast. I had some porcelain figurines I had given my wife, two little dogs and a cat, which Manuel had bought at a great bargain, and I was taking them to the plaza to sell. I went to my brother and said, "Shall we go to the plaza? I'll go ahead because I want to sell these, and you know it's best to get there early."

"Yes, *hombre*, you go ahead and I'll catch up."

I had no more than walked to the market, greeted some friends, and set out my wares, when my sister-in-law María came up and said, "Listen, Roberto, you'd better go to your aunt's house in a hurry because she's bleeding all over and is very bad."

I imagined that it was one of those hemorrhages from that place where she was sick, so I said, "All right, but I've got to take care of this now. It won't take long."

A woman stopped to look at the figurines.

"Come on," María said, "run, hurry."

"Wait a minute," said the customer. "What is the least you will take for these?"

"Give me a *peso* for everything. You can see what a bargain you're getting."

"All right, it's a deal. Now go ahead." And I ran, leaving María far behind. When I arrived there was a crowd of people in the courtyard, and they all stared at me. This annoyed me very much.

"Excuse me, let me get through, please, let me pass." Some of the older people made way for me and I reached the door of my aunt's house and found my brother.

"What happened? Have they taken my aunt, or what?"

He said, "No, brother, she is in there."

"Is she dead?"

"Yes, she is dead."

I went in and saw her. It was a very sad sight because she had died in much pain and in a way more wretched than the deaths of any other members of my family that I can remember. She was stretched out, face down.

I went over and touched her chest. She was very cold and I began to tremble. I could imagine the desperation she must have felt at the hour of her death. And I said, "*Caramba*, brother, look, here is the last of the Vélezes. She has gone, poor little old lady. What a sad way to die, all alone. Think of the contrast with her life. She always had her house full of people whom she was taking care of, and now no one."

I felt very much like crying, but I couldn't. I don't know why. I felt ashamed, thinking that my brother might take it badly, although he seemed relatively calm. I thought it would be hypocritical to cry.

"Ah, thank God she is at rest," I said. I had asked God to heal my aunt, but that if it were His will to take her, that He would not let her suffer very much. "And just look how quickly she has died. What shall we do? I only have forty *centavos* in my pocket."

"Yes, what shall we do?" Manuel asked. "Who's going to take charge of all this?"

"I will, brother, who else?" Then I asked him for five *pesos* for the bus and hurried to my godmother's house to see if she would lend me some money. But when I got there, my godmother had just gone to pay us a visit, so I left a message for her and went back to the Panaderos *vecindad*.

By this time someone had picked my aunt up off the floor and laid her on the bed. They had cleaned off the blood, and a woman, one of those old hags, had mopped the blood off the floor so that it looked a little cleaner. The only ones there when I arrived were my brother and my Aunt Prudencia and a couple of women who were my Aunt Lupe's friends.

My brother left to see about the funeral and in a little while my wife and my godmother arrived, bringing my son with them.

"Don't come in, Andrea," I said, "because it might harm the boy."

"*Ay*, whatever you say."

"What happened, Roberto?" asked my godmother.

"What do you think, godmother? The last one left to me of my mother's family has gone. And she died in such a miserable way that it hurts me. And, look, now we need money for the burial."

I brought only a hundred *pesos* with me," she said, "but I have another hundred and fifty *pesos* at home." I accepted the loan of 250 *pesos*, but I told her, "Look, I don't expect to have any money until December, and I'm not sure of that yet."

"What about your brother?"

"All the poor fellow has right now is ten or fifteen *pesos* in his pocket. So what are we going to do?"

"At least you have the two hundred and fifty *pesos*. Here are a hundred, and I'll go home right now and bring the other hundred and fifty." When she left I said to my wife, "Look, Andrea, here are seventy *pesos*.

Take the boy to Dr. Ramón and buy the milk and whatever else you need. And send a telegram to my sister Consuelo." I wondered if we should also notify my sister Marta in Acapulco, but I decided that with all those small children she wouldn't be able to come anyway, and the news would only make her unhappy.

By this time my aunt was already in the coffin. When Gaspar returned from the hospital, where he had been to get the death certificate, I said, "*Hombre,* what happened? Who brought this?"

"I did, *Señor* Roberto," he said. "It was the cheapest one I could find. At first the fellow at the Burial Agency wanted six hundred *pesos* for the complete service, with a hearse and a bus and everything but I told him, 'Six hundred! Excuse me, but I haven't got that kind of money. It's a lot for a man like me. I'm going where it will be cheaper.' So he called me back and said, 'All right, seeing it's you, I'll do it for four hundred.'"

Gaspar began to cry. That man was always crying! It made me angry. Honestly, I felt it wasn't the man who was crying but the hypocrite.

"Calm down, Gaspar, I feel her loss more deeply than you and I feel like crying too. But you don't gain anything by crying. What we have to do is get things done."

"Well, I brought the coffin," he said.

"Did you pay something down?"

"No. They told me at the Agency that as I was so poor they would give me until Monday to get the money together."

"It is Saturday now—three days of mourning for my aunt. All right, four hundred *pesos* is less than I expected."

Matilde and Pancho had offered to take up a collection among the news vendors. At about seven o'clock

Pancho's sister came in and I said to her, "Will you do me a favor? Go buy me some flowers and some candles for my aunt."

"Yes, gladly." I gave her thirty *pesos* and she brought me back sixty *centavos* in change because the flowers and candles cost twenty-nine *pesos* and forty *centavos*. I waited for Matilde's return to get some money to buy coffee, sugar, bread, and charcoal and to get some *chinchol* to spike the coffee for the mourners.

By nighttime, we were ready to begin the wake.

Consuelo

"*Señorita Consuelo Sánchez, Avenida del Sol, Nuevo Laredo.*" The telegram was short: "Come by plane if you can. Aunt Guadalupe died this morning."

You cannot imagine the shock it gave me. I had expected this blow, but I had trusted that when it came I would be there in time to say good-bye. After I read the telegram several times I sat down at my beloved typewriter. Usually it comforts me; it is the thing that brings self-respect and order to my life. But now I felt depressed, rejected, vastly alone. Two days before, on November 1, All Soul's Day, when I took my four nieces and nephews to church, I had knelt before the altar and had begged Christ to let me see my aunt before her end came. Then I looked directly at Saint Martín on his marble pedestal surrounded by lighted candles and I said to him, "Brother Martín of Porres, if it is true that you can perform miracles, I challenge you to heal my aunt—overnight. That is the only thing that will make me believe in you."

Saint Martín didn't take up my challenge and now I scolded him, "You are bad. I don't love you. You revenged yourself. Why? Why? I prayed so hard."

What can I say to express the pain that has drained away the last drop of joy from my heart? I have never been able to accept death the way it comes to people in my class. We are all going to die, yes, but why in such inhuman, miserable conditions? I've always thought there was no need for the poor to die like that. Their struggle is so tremendous . . . so titanic . . . no, no, it isn't fair. They can be saved. I refuse to resign myself to death in that tragic form.

There are authors who have written that the Mexican cares nothing about life and knows how to face death. There are jokes and sayings and songs about it but I would like to see those famous writers in our place, undergoing the terrible, hideous sufferings we do, and then see if they are able to accept the death of any one of us with a smile on their lips, knowing that the person didn't have to die. It's all a big lie. The way I see it, there's nothing charming about death nor is it something we have become accustomed to because we celebrate *fiestas* for the dead or because we eat candy skulls or play with toy skeletons.

Maybe the older generation did have a philosophy of not attaching great importance to death, but I believe that was the result of the suppression they were subjected to by the church. The church condemned them, in their minds, by making them believe they were worthless and that they could achieve nothing here on earth, that they would get their reward in eternity. Their minds were completely crushed and they had no hopes or illusions of any kind. I mean to say they were dead while still alive.

Nevertheless, when my aunt lost her only son and when my Uncle Ignacio died, she cried a lot and even had fainting spells. No, the death of a loved one is not accepted, anyway you look at it.

Life holds no pleasure for me anymore. I expect nothing here in my *tierra*, my own land. Why do we insist on carrying on that absurd masquerade, the gigantic lie that hides the real truth here in this "republic" of Mexico? "We, the Mexicans," amid "this prospering beauty with its politically strong, economically solid foundation . . ." Oh, yes, we are making progress. We are advancing in technology and science; the steel structures are rising over the corpses. Everybody knows that the peasants and the poor in the cities are being killed by starvation or other means . . . that they are being weakened. An entire generation is disappearing in an unforgivable fashion. I can no longer bear to see how they are humiliated and how they die.

Now my *viejita*, my little old lady, is dead. She had lived in a humble little nest full of lice, rats, filth, and garbage, hidden among the folds of the formal gown of that elegant lady, Mexico City. In that "solid foundation" my aunt ate, slept, loved, and suffered. She gave shelter there for a *peso* or two to any brother in misery, so she could pay her extravagant month's rent of thirty *pesos*. She swept the yard every day at six in the morning for fifteen *pesos* a month, unplugged the drains of the *vecindad* for two *pesos* more, and washed a dozen pieces of laundry for three. For three times eight cents, North American, she kneeled at the wash tub from seven in the morning until six at night. Besides all this, to be sure of something to eat, she would go from neighbor to neighbor minding the children for a mother who had just given birth, washing dishes and diapers, or scraping floors with steel wool and sandpaper, in return for which she might receive a *taco* which she would share with her *compañero*, Gaspar, or with some other hungry person. She even managed to find something to feed her dog.

It would have been absurd to call her "saint" but that's what she was. So gentle, so kind, so meek . . . she was incapable of insubordination to her masters, even to ask for the help to which she had a right. She was always ready to obey, always ready to serve. She revered the designs of God, unquestioningly following His commandments. Saints become saints because of their suffering. Well, she suffered martyrdom from the time they named her Guadalupe. To me she was both a saint and a mother. How can we have been so unmindful of her desperate need? Mexico, how can I love you when you devour those as defenseless as she?

Now we are free of that burden. She who was born "when the peaches were ripe . . . in the year . . . figure out how long ago it was, old man," she would say to my uncle. She who traveled with the guerrillas in the revolution, washing and ironing for "my General with the earring, my General Angeles . . . he was very particular." She, the last link to our dead mother, is now gone, slipping away from the edge of our lives along which she had passed on tiptoe.

I rested my head on the typewriter for a long time. The children paid no attention to me. They didn't even notice that I was upset. Mariquita, the eldest, who was fourteen, was washing her clothes and singing. Conchita, the youngest, sang, too, as she did the dishes. Alanes, the twelve-year-old was sweeping, and Little Domingo, ten, was out playing football. Manuel's children were so used to seeing people suffer that they set up a wall of indifference to shut off feeling. I tried not to be angry with them. Poor little orphans! They suffered so much to get so little. Knowing what future their lives would take if they were left in their father's house, I brought them back to Nuevo Laredo with me. So there were four others to share my meager typist's earnings. How I wanted to help them have a better life and how difficult it has been!

I thought of how badly my brothers had behaved toward my aunt, she who had given Manuel a home when he had married his first wife and who had taken in Roberto from prison when our father would not touch him. Two weeks before, in Mexico City, I had asked Roberto very specially to write me about her. That was after I had taken her to the doctor, who said she needed an operation and analysis to find out whether she had cancer. I was angry with everyone for not telling me sooner, for waiting until everything was over.

I imagined my aunt on her death bed, giving her blessing to everyone except me, asking for her "Skinny," which was the odious nickname that my father had given me in childhood. My father would never have anything to do with my mother's family, because of their drinking. Yes, my aunt and my Uncle Ignacio used to drink at night to forget their day's labor and their poverty. But at least there was love in their house and a refuge for me, when my own father drove me out. I pressed my hands against the pain in my head and asked, "Why didn't they let me know before she died? I would have gotten there. Ay, dear God, how bad people are!"

It was Sunday and the bank was closed so I borrowed

money from a neighbor for my ticket and a telegram: "Leaving by bus at two. Meet me." It was not until Mariquita saw me folding my black dress into my suitcase that she asked, "Are you leaving, aunt?"

"Yes, can't you see that I'm packing?" I was angry with the children for not even asking what had happened, so I didn't bother to tell them why I was going away. I gave them the 125 *pesos* for the week's expenses and warned them, "Be very careful. I don't want to find any accidents when I come back. You know that you have to lock up at night and not let anyone in. Nobody has permission to go anywhere. Mariquita, if you can prepare breakfast and dinner and get to school, go; if not, let them know you'll be absent—or figure out yourself what to do. I don't want any more problems."

I put on my make-up carefully and took my full-length red coat. I wore my dark glasses for I was barely able to keep from sobbing. I waited for the bus to leave and finally it pulled out at 2:45.

Along the way, I felt as though I were suffocating. Thinking that the change in altitude was making me feel faint, I tried to distract myself by writing down my thoughts, but I was unable to concentrate. I wanted to cry but I said to myself, No, don't! How angry I felt! I'll tell them a thing or two . . . but I must try to remain on good terms with my family. My little queen . . . how you must have suffered! That's enough . . . I've got to stop torturing myself. I looked up to heaven and begged that they would at least wait to bury her when I got there.

Fortunately my neighbor, a young man, started a conversation with me. He looked a few years younger than I, about twenty-two, or so.

"On a vacation?"

"Yes."

"For pleasure?"

"Yes, for pleasure."

I talked with him gladly although I had to turn toward the window now and then to free a tear. We introduced ourselves. He was a law student in his second year at the university. When I heard he was from the north of Mexico I was relieved. Northerners are more reliable and treat women better. By the time we arrived in Monterrey we were friends. He invited me for a cup of coffee and I accepted. I didn't care what I did; the important thing was to distract myself from my thoughts.

Finally my neighbor went to sleep and I let the tears come pouring down my cheeks unchecked. I couldn't get my aunt out of my mind. I reproached myself a thousand times for not having written to her. I didn't because I had no money to send and I always imagined the moment when she would open the envelope and find it empty. And when I had a little money, I thought that if I sent it, she'd use it for drink. I also felt that she had behaved a little badly because she didn't want to come and live with me in Nuevo Laredo. I was continually asking her because I needed her. I was hurt, but the last time I saw her, two weeks before, as we were saying good-bye I had consoled myself with the thought that she felt close to her *compañero*, Gaspar, and mentally I thanked him. At least she is not alone, I thought. I stood before her and said, "Give me your blessing, little mother. I'm leaving now, but we'll see each other soon." As I knelt down besides the bed where she was sitting, I noticed that there was only a straw mat on the bedsprings. I said, "I've been wanting to buy you a mattress for such a long time! I hope I can, soon . . ." She made the sign of the cross over my head and kissed me on the cheek . . . the sweetest, softest kiss. I think it was the first and only time that she did a thing like that to me. I can still feel it, like petals of a flower that rested for a moment against my skin. She said, "Write, daughter, write. Don't be foolish . . . write!"

"Yes, little mother, in a few days I'll send you enough money so you can see a doctor. And you know what? I'll come back in December and take you to Guanajuato. You'll like that, won't you? And we'll take Gaspar. So get well!" I said this to her with all my love, even though I doubted that there would be enough time or money. I now had Manuel's children to support. Nevertheless, I had hoped to be able to send my aunt something now and then. I gave her twenty *pesos*, which she put in the bosom of her dress and I turned and left quickly to hide my fear.

Just two weeks later, here I was, rushing to accompany her to her last resting place! The effort of holding back my tears made a hard bar of pain across my temples, and I began to hiccup in silent spasms. Soon I felt my neighbor's hand timidly brush my fingers. I thought to myself, The Mexican man! I need to get married . . . a companion is necessary at times like these . . . here I am, so alone, and so in need . . . My eyes moved along the faintly lighted, narrow aisle of the bus as I repeated to myself, Alone . . . I thought of Jaime, whom I had loved but could not respect, of Mario, whom I did not love, but ran off with, to revenge myself on my father . . . The man next to me kept up the gentle pressure on my hand. I mustn't forget where I'm going . . . but I don't want to think, to suffer any more. I wonder why life is so unhappy, especially for those of us who have nothing.

My neighbor leaned over and kissed my cheek. It was the tiniest of kisses. I looked at him out of the corner of my eye. Hmm, now you've made the test, I thought to myself. I know what you want and where you're heading. You can't fool me with your gentlemanly gestures. On the next try I put my hand between his mouth and my cheek and said, "Can't you sleep?"

He offered me a cigarette. I accepted with thanks. It gave me a chance to let some of my grief out in puffs of smoke instead of in sobs. The fact that he was aware of my troubles made things a little easier.

"You know what?" I confided. "What I told you this afternoon is not true. I'm not on vacation. I'm going to my aunt's funeral. She was my only relative on my mother's side. Now the whole family is gone." Even though I felt hesitant about talking, I began telling the whole story.

We continued conversing a long time. He told me about his grandmother, who was very sweet. He spoke of the differences in character between himself and his friends at the university, of how he admired the prudence and good conduct of girls like the ones who worked at Sears and Sanborn's, and about the parties he goes to, where he behaves frankly and openly like a northerner without caring what others will say. Each of us discussed our social contacts in Mexico City. Finally we stopped talking and I rested my head against the left side of my seat. After a few minutes he kissed me again on the cheek. I pushed him away but before I knew it his lips were on mine. I pushed him back harder thinking, That is as far as you are going to get. I drew quite a distance away and remained with my back turned to him until my leg fell asleep. Then he said, "Why don't you lean against my shoulder?" I rested my head on his shoulder, prepared to jerk it away if he annoyed me again, but he didn't and soon he was asleep himself.

At the next stop my friend invited me to have supper. He made some jokes at which I laughed and by the time we got back on the bus he had become "my faithful servant." He continued discussing a lawsuit he was working on. Like many law students, he was already acting like a lawyer, taking on their mannerisms and personality ahead of time. I smiled at his presumption and said, "Pardon me, I'm just a plain stenographer." He seemed to get the idea and stopped pushing his lawyer's shingle into my face.

Finally, everybody was asleep and the bus was silent. I was the only one watching the road. The driver's maneuvers were like bullfighter's passes when he went by trailer trucks on curves and wove in and out of lanes with cars coming from both directions.

Around five in the morning I began to feel terribly hungry. This was strange as I almost never notice hunger. I squeezed my stomach, closed my eyes, and tried to sleep, but the empty feeling pushed upward like a stick. My neighbor awoke and insisted on giving me some bread, and I tore off a piece and put it in my mouth. It felt like a piece of paper falling into a dry well.

We entered the State of Mexico and my companion got off at Tlalnepantla. Before he left, he wrote his address in my address book and said, "Write me."

"Of course," I said.

Tlalnepantla . . . my Uncle Ignacio's favorite place for eating a *taco placero* on Sunday among the crowds of people. My uncle, the news vendor, who never could get together enough money to visit Texcoco, where he was born. I closed my eyes on Tlalnepantla.

Then we came into the blossoming new *Ciudad Sate-*

lite, where people slept in their warm soft beds inside comfortable houses with not a fraction of a second's concern about the poor huddled outside. Again I thought, Mexico! At what a high price you are building yourself up!

It was after 8 A.M. when we pulled into the terminal. I had no strength to carry my suitcase. I did not want to get to my destination. I felt cowardly. As I was leaving the terminal a boy in a threadbare jacket practically pulled my suitcase out of my hands and said, "Anything you want to give me?"

"Give you for what?"

"For carrying your suitcase."

I got angry and was going to tell him off when a pair of policemen appeared and said, "Don't you know that grabbing packages is forbidden? Where do you work?" The boy's fear was evident as he began to explain to the police. I gave him fifty *centavos* for the bad time he was going to have.

I got a taxi and told the driver to take me to No. 33, Street of the Bakers. He seemed surprised at the address I gave him and kept trying to find out where I came from, but I was crying and couldn't speak. He said, "You must be bearing a load of grief, to be coming crying like this." That small drop was all I needed for my cup to overflow. So I told him what I had come for and his sympathy gave me strength to get to my destination.

PART
II

The Wake

Roberto

▨▨▨ **M**y aunt's associates were the very poorest —pure bums, drunks, old hags, thieves, *chinchol*, and *pulque*-drinkers. And they were all at the wake. I met friends of hers who had known my mother very well. They did not have much to say, just, "Ay, *negro*, we are very sorry."

"Who would have thought it?"

"I saw her just yesterday."

"But that's life. Sooner or later, poor or rich or powerful, we are all going there and we hope she'll make a little room for us."

"*Negro*, you know how badly I feel. Forgive me if I can't help you very much, but here is a little bit."

One of those who came in was more drunk than the others. He wore a coat that was a coat in name only, all torn and dirty, and a straw hat that was no more than a brim. His beard was filthy and his nose dirty and running. He drank a lot and talked and talked. "I'm going to stay with you, *Señor* Roberto, all night, and you'll see how good I am at a wake."

In a little while another came, disheveled, drunk, and bearded, wearing denim pants full of holes and shoes with only the tops left. The women wore clothes that were patches on top of patches, and even then their skin showed through. Each one who came into the room covered her head with her shawl or whatever piece of cloth she had brought. They came, heard the account of my Aunt Guadalupe's death, crossed themselves, prayed an Our Father and an Ave María and left. And as they left, "*Hombre,* here, I don't have any more but take it," and they gave me some money, a five, a twenty, a half *peso,* a few *centavos.* It meant taking a glass of *aguardiente* from their mouths, but they left their pennies for the old lady who had sheltered them in her little house. This tore at my heart. We didn't get much from them but I saw their sincerity. There were no crocodile tears among them.

It was my unpleasant duty to tell my father the news. I called him on the phone and said, "Imagine, *papá,* what has happened. My aunt has died."

"*Ay, caray,*" he said, "look at the situation I am in, so far behind . . ." And he began to tell me his troubles. I saw that I couldn't ask him for help because he was very pressed for money himself. Before he hung up he said, "If I get over there in the afternoon I'll see what I can do."

"That's fine, *papá,*" I said. I doubted that he'd come. I don't remember when my father has ever visited my aunt's house.

I went back and that bastard Gaspar was there. "Have you eaten?" I asked him.

"No, Roberto, but I'm not hungry. What I want most

is my old woman. My pretty little mother is gone. The people here say that I finished her off, but who should know better than you what really happened? I never struck my old woman." His words sounded so sincere that for a moment I felt sympathy for him. "Gaspar," I said, "take this *peso* and buy me some cigarettes, and get some for yourself."

While I waited I went over to a little grocery store and bought some bread and cheese and made myself a sandwich. I was eating it when Matilde came over.

"Listen, *negro*, have a cup of coffee."

"No, honestly I'm not hungry. Give the men the coffee with some alcohol, though most of them are going to want the alcohol straight. Let them have it as long as it lasts."

Gaspar returned drunk. Instead of buying the cigarettes he went and bought a *peso's* worth of alcohol. The drink had made him a little crazy. He saw the people praying and keeping vigil at the coffin, and said, "What are they doing in here? Let's go outside." Everyone ignored him.

"*Hombre*, Gaspar, please show some respect for the body of my aunt."

"Yes, *Señor* Roberto, whatever you say." And he would calm down for a little while, but then he'd start again. "Let's get out of here. What do you all want? When she was alive no one came to visit her, and now everyone is here crying. Bastards, hypocrites, go to hell!"

"Don't pay any attention," I told them. "He feels the death of my aunt, though not so much as I do, and besides he has been drinking." After a while he started in on me.

"No one gives orders here except me," he said. "This is my house"

"All right, Gaspar, all right, it's yours for the moment, but once my aunt is buried with proper respect, you'll have to get your things together and be on your way, because you have absolutely nothing here. This is not your house and never will be."

"Now we see who's giving the orders around here. My queenie newly dead and already you people are sharpening your claws. You're all like vultures, waiting for it to be over so you can take her things."

"Calm yourself, Gaspar. You are going to get me angry and then I'll sock you one."

"Go ahead, here's my chest." And he opened his shirt.

"Look," I said, "you're offending the corpse. You're showing no respect. Now it's up to me to get you out of here."

He said, "You don't say so! I've worked hard and my old woman left this house to me and now you come with strong hands and try to get me out. But it won't be easy, you'll see!"

"We'll see, all right." I grabbed him by his clothes and took him outside. I propped him against the wall and sat down where I could keep an eye on him. I was fed up with the guy. Out of respect for my aunt, and because it was a rare thing in my life to be insulted that way, I didn't feel angry. My grief was deeper than my anger. At that moment my only aim was to give the last member of my mother's family a decent burial. I watched the little procession of visitors that came and went through the door. I felt content that my aunt had her mourners, her flowers, and her candles.

Manuel

T HE bonfire that lit up the yard in front of my aunt's house gave little protection against the cold and the sharp night wind to the people gathered there. Leaning against the rough wall of wooden boards reinforced with pieces of flattened tin, Julia's daughter Yolanda hugged her two children close to her, trying to cover them with her ragged red cotton shawl. The backs of her shoes were doubled under to form soles, and her clothing, like her children's, was old and torn. A boy whose shirt was black with dirt sat in front of the fire, his head between his knees and his hands hanging at his sides, looking resigned to the sad reality of his miserable life. My brother Roberto, different from the rest because of his neat appearance, was sitting on the edge of a yellow wooden bench with two men I didn't know. Near them, huddled together on sheets of paper on the ground, trying to escape the piercing wind, were four other men in soiled shabby clothes. All four of them were drunk. Gaspar was in the doorway, swaying and holding on to the door frame for support. He stepped aside to let me pass.

Inside the narrow room was the open coffin. It was just a large box lined with cheap gray cloth. On the thin pillow filled with sawdust, under the sad yellow light of a small bulb hanging directly above it, my aunt's wrinkled face looked sick with use and neglect, and with a kind of boredom. Poor little old woman! Her eyes were slightly open and her toothless mouth was nothing but a black hole that seemed to be mocking us. The veins on her yellow-green forehead bulged, and I could clearly see the bruise she received on her left cheekbone when she fell.

There was a wreath of lilies and four candlesticks, one at each corner of the coffin. The tiny flames of the candles flickered as if they were burning against their will. Beside each candlestick stood four men, all poorly dressed, with sad faces and folded arms. This was the guard of honor, the last homage given to my aunt by her humble friends. They looked like characters from the court of miracles.

A few women squatted in the tiny space inside the kitchen door, some dozing and others talking in low voices. Laura, who smelled strongly of alcohol, said, "Ay, Señor Manuel, it's a good thing you came. If you could have seen how rude Gaspar has been! I didn't think your brother could stand him much longer."

Outside, Gaspar was listening and shaking his head. I went over to Roberto and asked him, "Say, brother, did this guy get stubborn?"

"Yes, but it's because the alcohol's gone to his head. Leave him alone, he doesn't know what he's talking about."

"But what did he say?"

"He said, 'Now I'm left with nothing. This funeral cost me four hundred *pesos* and you don't even appreciate it. After all my hard work!' So I said to him, 'Cost you what? Look, you'd better shut your mouth,' and I grabbed him and took him outside."

"You did right, Roberto. What a bastard! To claim that he paid for the funeral all by himself! What do you think of that?"

Gaspar stood swaying in front of us, trying to stay upright. Laura offered me black coffee in a chipped mug with a broken handle.

"No, thank you, Laura, I've just finished eating."

She went down the row of people giving them coffee. One of the four men sitting on the ground stood up with difficulty and took a bottle from the back pocket of his overalls. "Now buddies, since there isn't any here, I brought some alcohol for my friends."

"Didn't you buy any?" I whispered to Roberto.

"Yes, but it's all gone."

"Well, send out for another bottle, so you can offer these poor guys a drink. They're starting to make remarks."

"All right, brother, but keep your eye on that jerk over there. He's a rough customer."

I looked at the pair of jailbirds that had just arrived. The big one was a known thief. "Yeah, he looks like an ape with that beard," I said.

"That guy was in a lot better shape inside the pen than out. Inside he kept himself nice and clean. Every day he had his shoes shined and money in his pocket."

Meanwhile, the fellow was saying to his pal, "Tell them who I am, Rodrigo . . . you tell them."

"No, brother, I know who you are, but don't go making our pals feel small," this Rodrigo said.

"No, I just want them to know who your friend is, because fuck my mother if I wouldn't rather spend a hundred *pesos* treating my friends than on myself. That's how I am . . . like a man ought to be!"

The others finally managed to shut him up, motioning toward my aunt's coffin to remind him she was there.

Gaspar heard the rumpus and, hardly able to walk, he goes over to this guy, takes him by the collar, and says, "Listen, somebody's waiting for you outside. Let's go."

"Hey, what's the matter with you? Stop pulling me or I'll make you a head shorter."

"You're not scaring me, you jerk, let's go!"

"Leave him alone," interrupted my brother, grabbing Gaspar's hand. "And you, *señor*, see if you can keep your mouth shut now, will you please? You're not in a barroom. Keep quiet or I'll throw you out."

The fellow started to sit down on the ground, and my brother came back and sat next to me. But then this character straightened up and began to punch the air at an imaginary enemy. As he jumped back and forth he said, "Which one was it? This one or that one?" After throwing lefts and rights and uppercuts for a while, he stopped dancing around and said, "I'm sick and tired of taking this crap, and that's the holy Lord's truth. If anyone would tell me which one it was, you'd see how long he'd stay alive." He held three fingers of one hand as if they were a knife and he was sticking somebody. This seemed to satisfy him, and, aware that his audience had not missed a motion, he sat down saying, "You know me, Rodrigo. You know who I am." My brother and I looked at each other and smiled.

Drunk after drunk kept arriving at the wake. Every one of them stopped to look at the body, and all of them, without exception, reached into their poor pockets and produced a few *centavos*, or a *peso* or two—whatever they could manage—for the clay plate at the foot of my aunt's gray casket. It was their contribution to the burial. And all gave from the heart.

A man began praying out loud, yelling like a peddler, "Ivory tower. Forgive her, Lord." And everybody answered, "Ivory tower. Forgive her, Lord." In the prayer for the dead you ask the Tower of David . . . I don't know why an Ivory tower has to be asked to pardon a dead person, but it wasn't the prayer so much as the way he said it, like a guy going around shouting, "Ice Cream! Ice Cream!"

During the prayers, Rodrigo and his big-shot friend got up and left, returning with their arms full of scrap-wood and chunks of old tires which they dumped into the fire. Who knows where they robbed it, but they went for more and kept feeding the fire until dawn. Thick black smoke, twisted like a woman's braids, floated up toward the sky and was lost in the night. Little by little the faces of all those who were sitting near the fire became covered with soot. From where I was sitting I could feel a soft warmth on my knees. All at once the wind shifted, and a guy who was sitting there with his head between his knees jumped back so his hair wouldn't get singed. It was a young fellow called Pugnose. When he tried to smile his dirty face became covered with wrinkles, as though he had smeared his face with soot on purpose and then dragged wet fingers across it.

"*Ay*, you were all saying 'Pugnose has gone and burned

himself,' weren't you? But it's not so. No sir, I may be stinkin' but I ain't dead!"

Everyone laughed. Then a man called Dirty Face put a few sticks on the fire, just throwing them any which way. The jailbird who had almost gotten into a fight with Gaspar stood up and said, "Hey, watch out, you horse's ass, can't you see you're going to choke the fire?"

"What kind of a dope do you think I am? I suppose you're going to teach me how to build a fire. I can build fires with my eyes closed. What do you know about fires?"

"Oh, so you want to start a fight, do you?"

"Anything you say. You don't think I'm afraid of you, do you? The bigger they come the dumber they are."

The other guy put up his fists and began to dance back and forth again.

"This horse's ass is crazy," Dirty Face said, and taking the sensible way out, he went and sat down, saying "Oh, well, it serves me right for putting my two cents in." But the other one kept jumping around all by himself saying, "Come on, come on, don't back out, put 'em up, you son of a bitch." He stuck out his chest and held his fists tightly against it, but his friends calmed him back.

"*Caray*, young man, there's no respect nowadays, is there, even for the dead."

I turned around to see who it was. The speaker was an old man who my aunt had given shelter to. I said, "No, *señor*, there isn't. The crap some people try to pull . . ."

"Yes, *hombre!* It goes to show you how much we Mexicans are lacking." He remained thoughtful for a long time and then addressed me again. "*Caray*, life is strange. Just this morning, as I was leaving for work . . . I shine shoes, you know . . . it was about seven-thirty, and I think your aunt had already been awake for a long time. She said to me, 'Your shoe rags look awful dirty. Leave them here and I'll wash them out for you.' So I said to her, 'Ay, Lupe, God only knows what it costs you to get up on your feet, and yet you want to wash. Woman! No, stay where you are. Washing indeed!' 'Listen to him,' she said to me, 'you call washing out a rag work! Go on, leave them here for me. As soon as it warms up a little I'll get out and wash them. Go on, go on . . . don't make me beg you!'

" 'Do you really feel well, Lupita?'

" 'No, not really well, but well enough to wash a little still. Anyway, I don't feel right about your giving me the two *pesos* every day for nothing.'

" 'What do you mean, for nothing? You were the one who did me the favor of letting me stay here. You let me have a little corner of your house. No, let's not even discuss it. But if you insist, I'll leave the rags, just so you can't say I'm trying to slight you.' No, your aunt did not look well to me, but I never thought when I got back I'd find her stretched out already. It made me feel real bad, you can imagine! And, I don't know why, I had a kind of premonition that I needed to get back early today. But I was still too late . . . may she rest in peace. Perhaps it is better that God took her away without her suffering more. Gaspar is the one who's going to miss her most. Where is he ever going to find another Lupita, who kept saving everything for him, who would take anything from him, who had a home all ready for him . . . where will he find another one like her?"

The man's voice sounded angry as he continued to speak. "When things start going bad for you they really go bad, and that's God's truth. Just listen to what happened to me this morning. I got to the customs house and went right to work: 'Shine, mister? Shine, young man?' Well, when I was working on my first customer, this son of a bitch from the bootblack's union came over to me and wanted to take my shoeshine box away from me!

" 'Oh, no, nothing doing, brother,' I said. 'What right have you to take away my means of livelihood?'

" 'You have to have a union card. Let me see your papers.'

" 'My papers? When I was born there wasn't any registry office.'

" 'Come on, don't get funny. Let me see your permit.'

" 'Permit? The only one I ask permission from is God Himself, not sons of bitches like you.'

"Well, we were just on the point of tangling when this bastard backed down. But I told him the next one who came around would get his head bashed. No, working in Mexico nowadays is a headache, I can tell you! They don't give the poor man a chance, dues here, payments there . . . a man doesn't know where to turn any more. Everybody, from the cop on the corner up to the highest government official are a bunch of scoundrels who abuse the people. Look at this! Ten *pesos* for one week's license. Now, you tell me if this is justice, young Manuel. I knock myself out just so I can hand over my ten *pesos* to them! That's why I couldn't throw more into the collection plate for your aunt. I had five *pesos*, gave three, and have two left. Well, God will take care of tomorrow. Right?"

"Right, friend."

At around eleven o'clock the man who prayed like a street vendor started up again. He asked for a holy candle, lighted it, took a rosary from around his neck, and began to yell "Ave María Purísima," and you could hear the mumble of voices answering in unison, "You who have conceived without sinning." He prayed through the entire rosary in his loud grating voice.

Gaspar, who was standing by the door, began to fidget nervously and said loudly enough to be heard by some of the mourners, "Oh! What a pain in the ass! Over and over, praying and praying . . . what pests!" But he shut up when he saw that several people were looking at him with expressions that could hardly be called friendly. The rosary lasted a very long time, or at least it seemed long to me, and I imagined it must have been hard on those who were kneeling. When the man finished praying, he said good-bye and offered his services to all. "Today for her, tomorrow for me," he said, and went home to sleep.

"What a lovely rosary, *Señor* Manuel!" Laura's eyes glowed with satisfaction as she bent over the coffeepot. "That was what I call a rosary! Not like we usually pray, any old way just to get it over with. I think even Lupe enjoyed it, if God gave her leave to hear it. A drop of coffee for you, *Señor* Manuel?"

"No, thank you, I'm not cold."

The good woman poured a healthy slug of tequila into her cup and sat down feeling really at peace. I noticed that after my brother brought the tequila practically everybody wanted coffee.

What a wake! That wake was something in itself just because of the kind of people who were there. It's sad to admit it but most of them were down and out drunkards. I won't deny that many of them really had affection for my aunt, but I believe most came because they were driven by necessity. They are a very special kind of people who live in a way that's hard to describe. I don't want to sound like a politician but they belonged to a Mexico that is disappearing.

Finally it all began to get on my nerves, and I said to Roberto, "Listen, brother, I think I'll go now."

"Sure, sure, go home and sleep, so you can get up early tomorrow and sell some more figurines. We'll need the dough."

I called my wife, who was with the women, and everyone said good-bye in loud voices. Neither María nor I said a word all the way home. We walked as fast as we could because of the cold, and when we got to the Casa Grande the janitress took an age opening up. We didn't stop shivering until after we got into bed.

The next day, Sunday, I was out in the market at eight-thirty in the morning. I had a hundred figurines in a carton and was anxious to get rid of them as fast as possible. As the market began to fill up with shouts and people, I peddled them at the top of my lungs: "Figurines, one *peso* each, get your figurines . . . why pay three *pesos* downtown? . . . get them for the living room, the dining room, the kitchen. Bring a little present to your sweetheart, your *mamá*, your wife . . . only a *peso*, while they last."

Slowly my carton emptied. At one o'clock I got some breakfast from a woman who sells chicken broth in the market. I had a plateful of soup for three *pesos*, four *sopes* at thirty *centavos* each, and a Pepsi-cola. As I walked to my aunt's house I met Pancho and Matilde, who were looking for me.

"Look, *Señor* Manuel, we collected a little money from Pancho's friends. And we were thinking that you have a lot of friends here too, so why don't you take up a collection?"

They handed me an empty shoe box and the death certificate. That left me with no choice but to face the bull.

"Say, Shorty, how about giving a hand to help me bury my aunt?"

"Sure, brother. Hey, pitch in for this buddy here, his aunt died and he has to bury her."

Everybody put his hand into his cash box and *peso* by *peso* I managed to get together a little pile. Frankly, it embarrassed me, and I didn't ask everybody or I would have collected a lot more. Finally I got to my aunt's house and handed over about a hundred *pesos* to Roberto.

"Hi, *mano*, did you make up the amount?" I asked.

"No, not yet. I had to take some out for flowers and for this and that . . ."

"Yaaa! What did you spend so much on?" Before I could stop myself I had shown my mistrust. My brother almost got sore, but he said, "Well, I took some things out of hock that were going to be lost."

"Oh, no wonder. You did right. It doesn't matter, I have some more here. What time are they coming for her?"

"Well . . . we were supposed to have paid up by twelve o'clock, and since it wasn't possible, now the funeral won't be until tomorrow."

And so we had to sit up with my aunt all Sunday night, too.

Exhaustion was evident in the faces of the two or three women who had not left the body even for a little while. There was hardly anybody to keep us company now.

Even the fire was a very small one. My buddy, Dirty Face, was still stretched out on the bare floor with nothing to cover him but the night.

This session was more or less a repetition of the previous one. The complaints against Gaspar by the women who lived in my aunt's house continued.

"Just imagine," Chita said, "one night he wanted to beat me, too, because I wouldn't give him a *peso* and a half I'd earned by washing a shirt! If it weren't for the little departed one he would have, and because she defended me he hit her! He called her an old so-and-so and she said, 'I suppose you're still a baby, wet behind the ears.' Then she said to me, 'He's going to kill me yet. He makes me so mad I'm going to die of it.' Gaspar threw me out into the cold, and there I stood, all alone with my babies, shivering in the cold. And to make it worse, I hadn't been able to feed them all day. When I got back from my job I gave them a little black coffee and a roll with a few beans and that was all they had dancing around in their little stomachs. I was saving the one and a half *pesos* for breakfast and that is why I wouldn't give them to Gaspar. I wouldn't anyway. Why should I? Thank God, a man passed by and saw me crying and said, 'What's wrong?'

" 'Nothing, *señor*, it's just that they threw me out with my babies and I have no place to go.'

" 'Come with me. I'm alone.' What could I do, in God's name? So I went with him."

Meanwhile, a sister of my Uncle Ignacio was saying to my wife, "Yes, sometimes one wonders where one's head is. Take Lupe, getting the itch at her age, involving herself with a character young enough to be her son. And on top of it, taking all that from him! Beatings, and going hungry . . . especially after the way my dead brother Ignacio used to take care of her."

At nine o'clock Roberto went off to my room in the Casa Grande, leaving me his overcoat. The hours went by monotonously in silence. The five or six people who were still there no longer spoke and just drowsed. Suddenly there was a loud thud on the floor inside. Gaspar had tried to stretch himself out on three chairs that were near the coffin, but he was so drunk that he fell off, cutting his head, sending the candles flying, and nearly knocking over the casket. As I helped him up, I said, "Gaspar, man, be careful! You cut your head! Laura, please, I brought a bottle of alcohol, would you see if you can find it so I can put some on this man's cut?"

She found the bottle, and it was empty. She gestured that Gaspar had already disposed of the alcohol . . . inside him. So I washed the cut with a little tequila. After that he spread some rags on the floor and, after giving the coffin a good-night kiss, stretched out and went to sleep.

From nearby, loud music could be heard, the Florida Twist. A party with dancing was in progress.

"How do you like that, Manuelito? Us here with our grief and they with their pleasure as if nothing had happened!"

"Yes, Laurita, that's how it goes."

Ten o'clock, then eleven, then twelve went by. The lights in the rooms of the *vecindad* went out one by one, until only one in the rear was left burning. That was the room belonging to Ana, the janitress, where moonshine was made and sold. A trash-picker came in. He was very dirty and carried a big sack on his shoulder. He went straight toward Ana's room and came out with a bottle in his hand. It wasn't until then that he noticed the wake.

He moved the bottle to the hand that was holding the sack, and turning his face up toward the sky, he crossed himself. Then he went out into the street to face his destiny—collecting trash and swilling alcohol.

A little while later, two more guys came in and headed for Ana's room. They realized that a wake was going on and they removed their straw hats, crossing themselves as they continued toward the back. As they came out with the alcohol, I could hear one of them saying, "No, brother, it's not like you say. Look . . . life and death are *comadres*, good *comadres*, and that's God's truth. Life is the rich and powerful *comadre*, and when she doesn't want something or somebody any more she gives it to her poor little *comadre*, Death, all screwed and half-starved, for her to take home . . . and then . . ." The voice faded out as they passed.

My people are ingenious, there is no question about it, I thought after they were gone.

At around two or three in the morning, my eyes began to close. I felt the night and the silence like a weight on my head and shoulders, pressing me down into the bench where I was sitting. After another hour of it I went home with my wife and woke my brother.

"It's a good thing you woke me," he said when I told him the time. "Consuelo is arriving at five and I have to go meet her."

"Consuelo is coming?"

"Yes, didn't you know?"

"No, not a thing. All right, go on, and be careful. Cover up good, it's cold as the devil outside."

My brother went off to the bus station to wait for Skinny and I got into bed. That blasted Skinny! Coming all the way from Laredo! I wondered if she would bring my children back with her. From the time she stole them away she hadn't once written to me about them or told me her plans. Nor did I go after her or do anything to get them to return. At first, when I found out that she was the one who had taken them, I was terribly outraged, and so was María. "That bitch is doing this just to screw me, not to do anything good for the kids," I said. "No, María, I'm going to give her the works." I really felt like taking her to court, and that's the God's truth. But I couldn't because it was a question of kidnaping and that meant a lot of years in jail. After all, she was my sister. I couldn't do that to her.

When I got to thinking more calmly, I decided not to do anything at all; I'd let her keep them just to punish her and to cure her once and for all of that protective mania she had for them. And at the same time I'd cure the kids of wanting to be with her. Two birds with one stone. She always said she loved them, adored them. Why? Because she didn't know what children were like. Once they didn't obey her, or broke the dishes and the furniture, knocked the plaster off the walls, and began to ask for things, she'd come running here to dump them on me. So I let her keep them in order to cure her forever. And I wanted my kids to realize that the treatment they got at home, even though it was no prize package, was fairer and more equal than what they'd get from their aunt.

Consuelo always acted like she was the queen and they were her subjects. She put them to work and even made my son Alanes do the dishes and iron her dresses and underwear. A twelve-year-old boy! Was she trying to make him a fag? When he was little I worried about him because he liked to play with dolls. Then I caught him

Consuelo

As we turned into the Street of the Bakers, I told the driver where to stop. He asked me in amazement, "Here?"

"Yes, here," I answered.

The scene in front of my aunt's *vecindad* will always be engraved on my mind. It made me suddenly realize the truth about poverty, exposing its raw ugliness openly to the eyes of the world. The red brick wall of the *vecindad* framed a group of ragged beggars huddled near the entrance. Some were standing, their lowered heads covered with long matted hair full of lice and filth growing down into stiff, spiny beards. Their round, reddened, motionless eyes and open mouths had the idiot expressions of alcoholics. Others were sitting on the sidewalk with their knees drawn up, shrunken into themselves, or huddled together, for protection from the cold. Still others with no shoes and with crusts of filth covering their feet were lying asleep on the pavement. Nothing mattered to them. After all, to whom did they matter?

As I was taking out the money to pay the driver, a face appeared in the window of the taxi. It had a flattened nose, a toothless mouth, features swollen with alcohol into a faceless blur. The hair and beard were tangled into a single ball of filth. "Little boss," it said, "give me five *centavos* for a treatment. What do you say, little boss?"

The driver did not answer and turned to stare at me. I said in a sharp tone, "Don't give him anything if you don't want to. Get out of here." His attitude annoyed me. What could those poor things do to him? Besides, I thought to myself as I got out of the cab, these are my people.

The alcoholic breath of all those beggars reached me as I passed through the entrance. At the rear of the *vecindad* the neighbors were kneeling as usual before the wash tubs, scrubbing clothes, cleaning bird cages, or washing dishes. Everybody looked at me in suspense, as if waiting to see whether I was going to scream. Nobody approached me or spoke a word. I suddenly thought, They have taken her away! They didn't wait for me!

I began to feel dizzy, but I forced myself forward. There was nobody outside the door of my aunt's house except one of the adopted nephews she had taken care of. Nobody else. A feeling of infinite sadness came over me, as if I had come to the edge of a desert and found nothing.

I went in through the little kitchen to the doorway of the inner room where my aunt had slept. "This is where you used to live, little mother . . ." Now the room was empty. They had taken out the wardrobe, the bed, everything. All that was left were her saints. Her coffin, resting on two benches, was in the middle of the room. It was the cheapest kind obtainable. I had expected it to have a piece of glass on the lid so I could see my aunt's face, but no, it was closed. There were four candles burning around the coffin and underneath, on the floor, was a cross made of powdered lime for the eternal rest of her soul. It is a custom to also place a pot of vinegar with chopped onion under the coffin to prevent contagion from cancer, but I didn't see it there.

I wanted to go all the way into the room but the smoke of the burnt wax hurt my lungs. I also could not forget that the body had been there for two days now and, having just come from a journey, I had to be especially careful. My aunt's nephew did not move until he saw that I was about to go in. "No, little sister," he said, "it is bad for you. You have just arrived."

I stood in the doorway, feeling the great silence contained within those four narrow windowless walls. I looked at the holy images my aunt had taken so much care of and it seemed to me that they, too, wanted to sleep an eternal sleep. The place where the bed used to be was as empty as my soul, in its loneliness. There was nothing now but that gray box, immobile as the floor under it and as my aunt inside it, her eyes closed forever, her ears not listening any more.

Leaning against the door frame, I spoke to her silently. Now, little mother, now rest. No more hunger, no more pain. Now you are at peace. I got here late, but here I am, little queen.

I was about to go in and caress the coffin when I felt a heavy hand, hard as a piece of wood, on my arm, and heard Catarina's hoarse voice saying, "Come on out here, Consuelo. It will hurt you, *hombre*. It was cancer, you know. Come to my house. You can cry and scream there if you feel like, but not here."

I turned around and saw Catarina and her step-daughter Matilde. Catarina was a stout, red-faced woman of about fifty, who had trouble breathing because of chronic bronchitis. Besides, she drank a lot. All of them did in that *vecindad*. Catarina's nose was swollen from alcohol. She had no upper teeth and her eyes were tiny and protruding.

Matilde was young, not over thirty, but she looked older than her age. She dressed in the typical way of that *vecindad*, in second-hand clothes that didn't fit and were faded or torn. That was the way my aunt had dressed, too. On this day, Matilde wore a black blouse and a crooked black skirt covered by a long, dirty apron. Her bare feet were in shoes that were much too large for her. She never wore a brassiere and she had the habit of crossing her arms over her breasts as she walked, bending forward so that her chest and stomach were practically joined. Matilde was ugly because her nose had been broken and was completely flat. She said she had had an accident, but my uncle once told me that her father had beaten her when she was little and had smashed in her nose. Uncle Ignacio was Matilde's mother's brother and he had known Matilde from the time she was born . . . My aunt was her aunt too.

The two women pulled me out of the house and into the yard. They seemed concerned about me. But I thought about how they had left my aunt alone in her hour of need and I felt my anger rising. I asked Matilde reproachfully, "Where's my brother Roberto?"

"You told him to meet you, so he went to the bus terminal. He should be back in a little while."

I said nothing and followed them across the yard. I felt as if I were floating, folding up in pleats, getting thinner and thinner . . . Everybody's eyes were on me, but nobody moved. There was a strange feeling of something unpleasant in the atmosphere. My knees were buckling as we passed the wash tubs. There was Julia's granddaughter, pregnant already, a kid of sixteen.

Catarina's house, No. 14, was in the rear of the *vecindad*. As soon as we entered, she offered me her only chair. The apartment was like my aunt's, one small room and a tiny kitchen. Here lived Catarina, Matilde's father José, Matilde, her present husband Pancho, her grandmother, and Matilde's two children. Catarina and José and Matilde's eldest child, a girl of about fourteen, slept in the bed in the back room. The grandmother slept crosswise at the foot of the bed. Pancho, Matilde, and her young son slept huddled up on the kitchen floor; it was so small they could't even stretch their legs.

Matilde wanted to get out of that place so that she could live alone with Pancho and "have room to turn over in bed," she said. She and Catarina fought all the time because when they got drunk Catarina's anger came out and Matilde had to defend herself. She was always at her step-mother's orders and, fighting or not, she stayed constantly at her side. It was a dog's life. Matilde looked for a room she could afford but there was none to be had.

Matilde was good. In spite of all her sufferings and privations she did not neglect her children. She never complained about her lot in life and gladly helped Pancho sell his newspapers or took her place at the little street-stand outside the *vecindad* where she sold slugs of brewed alcohol. She had never gone to school and was illiterate,

yet she learned to recognize some letters in the newspapers. Above all, Matilde had been good to my "little
old lady" and I felt a deep affection for her now.

The bad smell of the toilets in front of Catarina's
house reached me as I was sitting there. But what difference did it make? My aunt had lived here too. I looked at
Matilde and, trying to keep my voice from scolding, I
asked, "Why didn't you let me know sooner? Why?"

"Well," she said, "it happened so suddenly. She was
alone . . ." *Alone!* The word burned into me like a live
coal. I had consoled myself with the thought that my
aunt had died in bed, surrounded by people she knew.
"I think it must have been something like her liver
bursting, because she vomited a lot of blood." Matilde
continued, in her flat voice, "And when she fell she hit
herself against a brick and cut open her forehead . . . and
she just lay there . . . Pancho was the one who found her.
I said to him, 'Go see if my aunt wants a little tea or
juice.' Whenever I had a few extra *centavos* we would
buy her juice. So he went and found her lying in a puddle
of blood."

I felt horrified, as if a dagger were being forced through
my forehead, but they kept right on talking without even
noticing. Catarina said, "I told them, 'The police have
to be notified, so nobody can be accused of anything,
right?' Then those bitches, my *compañeras*, said, 'The
Red Cross has to be called to come and get her.' So I said
to them, 'Call the Red Cross my ass. Nobody is taking
a fucking thing out of here.' I told them off and Gaspar
went to notify the police, because she had an attack, you
know. There was a lot of blood. It stank something
awful."

I wanted to stop them, to scream or to cry, but all

I could do was clench my fists and curse inside me. *Christ! Yes! Lay it on! Here we are to take it! Why, Lord, why does it always have to be us, the ones who have nothing? Lay it on heavier, Lord! Send all you want.* I broke into a sweat realizing how powerless I was, just another poor Mexican who had nothing to fall back on at times like this. I wept and sweated with the pain of the Mexican essence inside me.

When I could speak, I said, "Matilde, didn't they give her any treatment at the hospital?"

"No. Gaspar told me they wanted fifteen *pesos* and said to take her away until he brought the money."

"I lent them bus fare whenever I had it," said Catarina.

"And I would give her money for her juice," Matilde added.

I felt that they were saying this as a warning, so I answered, "Don't worry, I'll pay back whatever my aunt asked of you. Did Roberto come to see her?"

"Yes," said Catarina, "that he did, and when he had it he brought her money."

"What about Manuel?"

"You know you can't count on that one for anything," said Matilde. "He was here last night, and it seems he helped Roberto raise money for the funeral. I helped them, too. We collected among all of us."

"And my *papá*? Did he come?"

"No. *Señor* Roberto told him, but he didn't come."

This made me very angry, and I said to her, "Yes, the great *Señor* Sánchez. The day he dies I won't come either . . ." I couldn't keep back my tears. I was the one who should have been with her. What a horrible thing it is to feel remorse!

"Now, now," said Catarina, "don't cry any more.

Lucky her, up there with the Lord. Poor us, left behind to suffer here. Now stop crying or you'll get sick."

"Do you have a little tea, Catarina, please? My stomach is hurting me."

Instead of tea they gave me a large glass of milk, a luxury in that household. All my scruples and resentment fell away at that moment. I recognized the love and understanding that existed among them in spite of their poverty-stricken lives. What would I have done in the same circumstances?

Catarina went on talking. "Don't cry, girl. She isn't suffering any more. Ay, some of these lousy old women around here said, 'I'm not going in there. It's cancer she had, I might get hurt.' They were afraid, afraid. And I told them where to go. I said, 'In any case you're going to end up screwed, either by this putrid *chinchol* that has us all ruined or from your own rotten souls. We were born to die,' I told them. 'If we're going to the devil anyway, why are we standing around like clowns? Get out of the way.' And I picked her up and put her on the bed and told the rest of them to fuck their mothers. Don't you want some more milk?"

I was affected by Catarina's words. She and Matilde were trying to be kind to me, but I had had enough milk and I put the glass on the table.

"Matilde, have they told Jaime?" I asked.

"No. We were afraid you might be angry if you came and found him here. So we decided to wait for you."

I thought of how my aunt had called Jaime "my dark one, my handsome little nephew." She told me, "Marry him, Skinny. Then he will accompany me to my final resting place when I die."

"Call him, please, Matilde. His number is on the corner of the calendar in my aunt's house."

"Ask him for money," said Catarina. "Don't be a fool."

Matilde went to the telephone in the little store outside the *vecindad*. While she was gone I asked Catarina where Gaspar was. She said that maybe he had gone to bring a priest. "To tell the truth," she added, "he's afraid to lay eyes on you."

Matilde came back, out of breath. "You've got to come and talk to him." I went to the telephone and picked up the receiver to hear again the voice that, years before, had made me fall in love with him.

"Jaime, I called to ask you to come to the funeral, because my aunt always thought a lot of you. She would have liked for you to come."

"All right," he said. "I'll come over. *Caray*, I hope I can get off from work."

I hung up and paid Matilde for the call. "Why didn't you tell him about the money?" she asked.

"Because he already knows he has to bring it. Let's go."

As we returned to the *vecindad*, Julia greeted me. "*Comadre*, you know how sorry I am . . ." She was the only one who had come up to express her sympathy. The other neighbors had withdrawn their friendship one by one because of Gaspar. All of them fought with him. Once Julia had hit him with a piece of wood. They couldn't forgive him for taking the place of my Uncle Ignacio, who used to say, "My wife is the center of my home." He had taken pride in being a news vendor and believed that "a man is a man who works at whatever God offers him."

I went back to sit at the door of my aunt's house. I

stayed there like a stone taking the sun and letting the wind blow over me the dust that I had always feared because it carried germs. Let it blow . . . let it dirty me! I wished that my soul could fly away like the dust.

I emerged from my stupor when I heard my brother's voice and felt his hand on my head. "Sister," he sobbed, and his tears fell into my hands. But I couldn't cry. I was angry and wanted to scold him. I wanted to say, "Roberto, couldn't Andrea have come to look after her in her last days? Do you remember when Andrea had her baby? My aunt was already suffering the horrible pains of that accursed sickness, but she would take the bus every morning and go to your house to take care of your wife. And, at night, tired or not, back she would go to her poor little hut to give Gaspar his supper. Yes, she was always on the run, taking care of this one and that one. And what about us? We neglected her, brother. What kind of people are we?"

I wanted to say even more to him but I said nothing at all, so as not to start a fight.

"*Ay*, sister, where were you?" asked Roberto, when he'd stopped crying.

"I'm sorry. I came another way."

I asked for Manuel. Calm now, Roberto answered, "He's at home. He was here with us all night." He tapped his stomach. "Say, sis, have you had breakfast? I haven't yet, and my stomach is hurting me."

"No, I had no time. Matilde gave me some milk."

"Do you want something else? I can send out for it."

"Send for anything you like." My brother gave me the impression that after crying he breathed easier, as though he had gotten rid of something bothersome. When my uncle died Roberto had said. "It's better this way." It had angered me then and I wondered whether he'd say the same of my aunt's death.

Roberto told me how he and Manuel and Matilde had raised the money for the funeral. I thought to myself, So she is going to be buried by charity too, like my Uncle Ignacio . . . like all of them." There wasn't a family in that *vecindad* that could bury anyone without taking up a collection. One family had kept the body in the courtyard for several days while they went around begging for money. The body had begun to smell already. Roberto and I happened to go there and when we heard about it we went to the Casa Grande to beg for money ourselves. And now my aunt, too . . .

"Do you need any more money?" I said.

"No, well, yes, only about thirty-five *pesos* that I spent on taxi fare looking for you."

I asked him, "Well, what time are they coming for her?"

"They should be here before noon. It's all arranged, except I still have to take the medical certificate to the undertaker's. I'll do it after I eat."

When Roberto left, Matilde and Catarina came over with Gaspar. He seemed frightened. I wanted to tell him not to be afraid, that I wasn't going to call him to account for having left my aunt alone. All I said to him was, "Gaspar, she's left us." He lowered his head and tears streamed from his eyes. I was not angry with him. What could he have done? A man who didn't know how to read or write, who lived beaten down by suffering and lack of proper food, who shared his *chinchol* with my aunt. What was he going to do now, all alone? I remembered what my aunt had said of my Uncle Ignacio. "What will become of this poor man if I die? He is alone, alone as an ear of corn in the field." Now it was Gaspar who was alone. I pitied him. Oh, I thought, my brothers will probably tear into him. The neighbors too, I suppose.

"Gaspar, where were you when . . . when it happened?" I asked.

Still frightened, he answered, "Me? In the market, with this one's husband." He pointed to Matilde. "You see, Lupita had been up early to sweep the courtyard and to help *Doña* Ana sell *chinchol* and she was resting in bed when I got dressed. I told her, "Get up, *hombre. Caramba!* Even if it's just to sew on my jacket button for me.'"

She said, "Soon. I'll do it soon," and I left. And on the way back Pancho came running up to me to tell me, "Lupita is dead!"

He began to cry as he spoke, "She's gone and left us, *Señorita* Consuelo . . . Do you know how much I had in my pocket when I found her stretched out on the floor? Twenty *centavos.* That was all I had." His sobs kept getting heavier. "God, not even enough for a bus . . . nothing for a doctor, or anything. It took me an hour and a half . . . I went to the police, walking without even knowing where I was going. I told the man behind the counter about it and he says to me, 'No, this isn't a police case.' And off I go again, back and forth, back and forth . . . How is a person supposed to know his way around those offices?"

"Gaspar," I said, "Dr. Santoyo told me they were going to give her a pass to be admitted to the hospital."

"Well, but they didn't give her a bed, because there wasn't one empty, or who knows what? Look, *Señorita* Consuelo, what happens is that we have no money . . .

that is why they treat us like that. Because if we did, you can bet your life it would be a different story."

I watched the tears run down Gaspar's cheeks and saw him clench his fists as he spoke, as though to crush his impotence but also to show the strength of his rage. I could see in him the pain of a man who feels powerless in the face of the accursed poverty that is defeating him. Usually men like Gaspar face up to every adversity and bear all the calamities that happen to them. But at moments like these they surrender and lower their heads. Gaspar gave in to his grief and I respected him.

After a moment, as he wiped the tears from his dark cheeks, he went on, "Where was I going to get the money from, *Señorita* Consuelo? I was without work. There is a lot of competition now, and my trade has been made cheap. Wherever you go downtown you can see the boxes of cheap shoes. They offered me fifty *centavos* a pair for nailing shoes and I am better off selling alcohol here. *Doña* Ana pays me two *pesos* a day for selling little bottles of her stuff out in the street and that's what my old lady and me were living on. But even so we had everything pawned . . . everything we ever bought: the iron, my *viejita's* dress, even my working tools. We had nothing at all. And in the hospital they wanted five *pesos*, then ten *pesos!* There we would go, my little old woman and I, step by step . . . she could hardly walk, but we kept on. When the pain took hold of her she would just lean against the wall and say to me, 'Look, man, I can't walk any more. I can't make it.' And I would say to her, 'Come on, don't give up. Aren't you a strong woman? Am I not here, or what?' And on we would go again, step by step."

He fell silent and I just sat there, lost in my own thoughts.

Prudencia, my aunt's former sister-in-law, came with two of her grandsons. A little later more of my poor cousins arrived. They all embraced me. "Consuelo . . . you know . . ." I wished that they would keep quiet. One of my aunt's many *comadres* arrived with a bunch of flowers. She embraced me and said, "You know we are with you in your grief, Consuelo." I did not answer. I thought, Yes, now you grieve. Why didn't you come to see her when she was alive? What is the good of it now?

Angélica, the only friend I had left in the Casa Grande, arrived dressed in black. She sat down next to me and squeezed my hands. "Here I am, Consuelo."

"Yes, Angélica, I know. In good times and bad, you are always there . . . my friend."

A little later Jaime arrived. I tried to hold down the resentment that the sight of him brought back. He had made me suffer very much. Upon entering he greeted everyone, making a polite little tour around the group. Ah, the middle class! Gaspar offered his hand, but Jaime ignored it to take the hand of Angélica, who was far better dressed than the others there. I had taken off my necklace, earrings, stockings, and colored jacket, and was wearing my plain black dress and my dark eyeglasses.

Jaime acted surprised when he saw me. He held out his hand. "Hello. How are you?"

"All right, Jaime. Thank you for coming."

"You are very thin. Why?"

"I don't know." Why did it seem strange to him? I've always been like this. I felt embarrassed and sad. Very few people had come. I had expected many more . . . at least all those to whom my aunt had given food and shelter. But no, we were very few. The residents of the *vecindad* behaved coldly. They walked past and looked at us, but no one spoke. Everyone who passed in front of the house covered his nose with a red handkerchief. They thought the color red helped keep the cancer from spreading.

In house No. 10 a fight was going on. Lucha's husband, Juan, was drunk as usual. He stood in his doorway, threatening the whole family and challenging his fifteen-year-old son to fight with him. Lucha came out sobbing loudly, and passed by, paying no attention to us. Wiping her tears with her hands and drying her hand on her skirt, she shouted insults at her husband. Everyone else just stood around and watched or went about their business as though nothing was happening.

Angélica said to me, "Consuelo, go over to Jaime. If you don't he'll say we left him alone and he'll want to leave."

I went up to where he stood aloof from everything and I said, "I'm sorry. It shouldn't be much longer."

"They only gave me two hours off."

"Jaime, you know these things take time. If I disturbed you by phoning it was only because my aunt liked you so much." I was nervous and upset.

Roberto came back. "Well, it won't be much longer," he said.

"Did you arrange for her to be buried with the rest of our family?"

"No, sis, it takes too much time." I was angry at that but Angélica calmed me.

Then I saw Manuel and María come in. What contempt I felt for them! Even their way of walking was scornful. Why had they come? To show off, no doubt; and so that everyone would say, "Yes, they did their duty." Manuel did not feel a fraction of genuine or even superficial grief. His jokes, his laughter . . . how I hated him!

My brother Roberto and a few others were keeping watch beside the coffin. When I saw them go inside the back room I thought, What a coward I am. Look at them next to the body, without fear. My brother is crying, poor fellow, and breathing in all the vapor that is rising less than two feet from him. And I? . . . At last I went inside, where my aunt was lying. The candles had dripped so much that the wax looked like a veil. I approached the coffin and caressed it as if I were touching the feet of Christ.

"*Mamita*, my dear one, rest in peace."

Prudencia pulled me outside. I went meekly to the corner of the kitchen where my aunt's dog, Chocolate, always slept and I began to pray. The truth was that I was afraid to stay near the coffin.

We could still hear *Señora* Lucha fighting with her husband. He was insulting her and trying to push her out and close the door. The little children were crying and the eldest son sat alone near the doorway, his head down, while his mother and father exchanged abuse.

I saw my brother Manuel lounging against the wooden wall of the new carpentry shop, chatting as usual, making jokes, chewing gum, and looking for all the world as if he were waiting to see if the horse he had bet on would come in first. Not for a moment was he nervous or upset. He was only an observer at whatever spectacle came his way. María, his wife, made me think of a gangster's moll, observing everything and remaining untouched by it.

I decided to speak to Manuel. "How are you getting along?"

He replied with his usual forced good humor, "I'm making out all right." He looked me over. "You're still very skinny."

Before I could speak, my sister-in-law said, "It's not so strange. She was always very delicate."

I turned my back and walked away. I couldn't stand them.

Later, at what he thought to be an opportune moment, Manuel walked over to me. Putting his arm around my shoulder like someone trying to make up with an enemy, he led me a little away from the group to confide a secret.

"Do you know what, sis? I don't think that the house and all the things that belonged to our aunt should be left to this guy Gaspar. Imagine, they say he used to beat her until she bled. How can we leave her things to him? We can sell some of them, and with . . ."

My aunt had not been laid to rest and they were already fighting over her pitiful possessions! I wanted to strike Manuel, to shout how vile and despicable he was. "Manuel, she is still here and you want . . . oh, how horrible." His crafty, Asiatic expression faded, and he said, "But it isn't right for this fool to stay here. He's just an idiot who's good for nothing."

"Yes," I shouted, "Just like you. You aren't worth anything either. I absolutely oppose what you suggest."

My brother couldn't have chosen a worse moment to show his venom toward my aunt's *compañero*. Gaspar had hit her? All right, she had loved him. It was her life. As in every marriage, they had fought, and if she had never complained of him it was because she was fond of him. Why should we take vengeance? At least he had offered her his company, which none of us had done.

Roberto called me aside and told me that he agreed with Manuel about Gaspar. "I've already told that fool he could stay here for a few days, while he looks for something else."

"Look, Roberto, I don't want to discuss this now, but I don't think she would have had the heart to throw Gaspar out into the street. He is a poor man. He is not prepared to take care of himself. How can we put him out?"

"But why should the things she cared for belong to him? He'll just sell them, and besides he was rough with her."

"Look, brother, you too fight with your wife. That's all they did. I want to do what my aunt would have done. As for her things, we'll see."

"This is why we didn't decide until you came. I could have gone ahead and gotten that fool out, but I wanted to know how you felt about it."

"So you did, and you would have been within your rights as an older brother. Thank you for waiting. You deserve credit for that. I'm proud of you."

"Good. I told them that they can stay in the house too. It's better that . . ."

"They? Who are they?"

"Matilde and Pancho. They are chasing after Gaspar to ask for the house. They said as soon as we carry her out they're going to see the owner, so I said I'd move them over and get myself a few *centavos* from them for making sure they got the house. After all, if I can help myself . . ."

At last I understood the reason why Catarina and Matilde were so friendly to me. "Well, we'll see. I want my aunt's house to stay as it is. We'll make arrangements later. Look, brother, what you are thinking is not right. You are strong and able to work. In comparison with Gaspar, you are better prepared."

I realized it was Manuel who had spoken through Roberto's mouth. Roberto was guided more by sentiment than by material things. It is true, as Manuel had told me, that "to be practical it doesn't do any good to get sentimental. It is better to sell some of her things and get a few *centavos* from the house." But didn't her kindness deserve some respect? Didn't the love she felt for the fruit of her labors, her wardrobe, her bed, her saints, deserve some honor? When she leaves should every trace of her also go? I know that everything is going to disappear, but wouldn't it be better to erase her footprints gently? Little by little?

Jaime called me. From the tone of his voice I knew he understood that I had been upset. "Come on. Let's go buy some flowers." I asked Roberto, "Is there time to go to the market?"

"Yes, but don't take long."

As we walked along, I remembered how Jaime and I used to go together to buy fruit. He must have been recalling it too, for as we passed a fruit stand he stopped to buy some tangerines which we ate as we went. Few words passed between us; we spoke mostly of our families and friends. We bought the flowers and hurried back. I gave the rest of the tangerines to Angélica and placed the flowers at the foot of the casket. By now there were several wreaths.

I recalled my aunt's little face when she used to arrange flowers for the Lord. In her entire life she never failed to offer them on holy days. She would say, "Here are your flowers, *Papá*. They are lovely, aren't they? I brought my Father His flowers." And she would cross herself. Now I was saying the same thing as I offered the flowers to her.

At that moment, Lucha's husband staggered in and asked drunkenly, "Where's the fight?" Then he left on his wobbly legs, threw his children out of the house, and shut the door. Julia came by on the way to the bathhouse with a bar of soap and a sponge in her hand. She stopped for a moment. "Consuelo, how are things going with you? I have a terrible problem. Guillermo is about to lose the television set, his great investment, and now I have to see if I can raise some money. Excuse me for not going to the funeral, but I have a lot to do." She went on her way. Another neighbor passed by with soap and towel. No explanation was necessary. She too would be unable to accompany us to the cemetery.

Catarina and Matilde both wanted to speak to me about the house and about my aunt's belongings. I didn't want to talk about it anymore and I walked past them and sat down in the sun to wait for the hearse. I recalled something my Uncle Ignacio had once said. "After all, we aren't going to take anything along with us. Nothing really belongs to us. It all remains here. We just go as we came—with nothing." How true were his words!

PART
III

The Burial

Manuel

r⊃r⊃r⊃ O_N Monday morning, the day of the
funeral, the sun was out, nice and warm. When I arrived
at my aunt's house there were about twenty-five or thirty
people standing around, talking about little things. My
sister Consuelo was there with Jaime, the shorty, her
eternal suitor.

"Imagine, Manuel," Matilde said to me, "your sister
says that Gaspar is going to stay here in the house with
everything."

"What! No, that's impossible. She must not know
how he treated my aunt."

At that moment Consuelo came over, and we stood
there looking at each other.

"*Hola.* How are you?"

"*Hola*, Sis, how have you been? Say, you look skinnier
than usual to me."

"No, I'm the same as always."

I made a sign to her to move over where we could talk without being overheard. "Say," I said, "is it true that you were saying that Gaspar should stay on in my aunt's house?" I tried to put my arm around her but she pushed it off.

"Yes, why?"

"But, man, that fellow treated Aunt Lupe very badly . . . they say—"

"Nothing but gossip." She cut me short. "Besides, I know what I'm doing. Nobody has more of a right than I to say what should and should not be done. The room and all the things go to Gaspar. He was my aunt's last husband and that's what she would have wanted."

"*Hombre!* Look, Consuelo, that may be what she wanted but our poor aunt is dead now. And Gaspar was a son of a bitch who hit her and who wanted to fornicate with her in front of people even when she was sick with a cancerous fistula. He treated her in an inhuman manner. Now, why should her things go to him? Why should the images of the *Niño Dios* that were in the family for eighty years, or the picture of the *Divino Rostro* that is sixty-nine years old and that had belonged to my mother and grandmother, be given to him? Those alone are worth over one hundred fifty *pesos*. And there are at least sixteen other pictures of saints and virgins. That drunkard would sell them one by one just to buy alcohol. He's nothing but a worthless bum."

Consuelo cut me off again saying, "Just like you. You're exactly the same so why are you so surprised?"

I was angry but I controlled myself. "But, look, with what we get for the things and for the transfer of the house . . ."

"No, I don't want any transfer money," she said.

"Look, please let me finish. All I'm saying is, with what the things bring . . . Man, my aunt in her lifetime never had any sign of distinction, any kind of privilege, at least let's give her a cement headstone in death."

"No sir, nothing doing! Things are going to be done the way my aunt would have wanted." And as she said this, she turned her back on me in a very impolite manner, leaving me with my mouth open.

That bitch! It was she and not my aunt who was doing the talking. She was just using my aunt as a pretense to get her own way. Even at the funeral my sister came around with the same hard feelings and that same conceit that because she knew shorthand and could write on a machine she had more rights. All her life she wanted to know more than I did so she could act superior. I'm not a genius, but I've been around a little more and I see things a little bit clearer and more objectively than she does. The truth is that she thought I was so much of a businessman that even in that sad situation I was capable of trying to make money for myself on those useless little things. Their sentimental value was much greater than their material value and all I wanted were my mother's pictures. I told her, "Look, Consuelo, you can come to the market and see how much I sell the things for. You handle the business of the transfer." But she wouldn't listen. She contradicted everything I said. She was cutting, high-handed, hard.

I sat down on the bench outside my aunt's house. The sun on my back felt good. People were standing around saying, "It's getting late and the undertakers aren't here yet!"

Finally a gray hearse arrived, a half hour late. Those guys from the funeral parlor came to do a job and cared nothing about keeping up appearances or anything. They were completely indifferent to the grief of the mourners. It was pure business. Right off, they wanted to be paid. Consuelo came over to me and said, "Listen, Roberto doesn't have enough money. He needs thirty-five *pesos*. Do you have any?" Jaime, the shorty, stuck his hand in his pocket at the same time I did and handed over twenty *pesos* to my brother. I gave the rest. Then two of the undertakers picked up the heavy candlesticks and carried them out. I looked around for a wreath but nobody had brought one. There were only a few withered flowers. And there was only one funeral bus. It was one of those old public buses, with seats in rows on each side of the aisle. The bus was painted black and in fair condition but inside it was very dirty.

It's a little ironic but even the dead have their status. The difference in price decides whether you travel first or second class. If you pay more, you get an elegant hearse, a fancy casket, a later model bus and the mourners are treated with every consideration. My aunt's funeral was the very poorest there is. She went second class right to the end.

A crowd of people, mostly children, began to get on the bus. Some women were carrying my aunt's little evergreen plants to put on the grave. Everybody was pushing and rushing around, children were whining to go with their mothers. It reminded me of the pilgrimages we used to make to the shrine in Chalma.

The bus filled up quickly and someone yelled, "No, no, the kids can't go. Just adults! All children get out!" Seats were set aside for the mourning relatives and when my name was called, I got on the bus with María.

I had not intended to go to the cemetery, but everyone expected me to so I did. The day I buried my first wife, Paula, I swore never to go to another funeral that was not my own. It's hard for me to describe what a cemetery represents to me. It is not a matter of fear but rather of pain, pain that is deep in the most secret part of my soul. I know myself. I know the kind of traumas I suffered from. Not only my wife's death, but my mother's and my *papá's* second wife, Alicia. I felt them all because my father blamed me for all of them. To this day I can't get his accusing voice out of my mind.

Look, death in itself is something very serious. It's nothing I'd make jokes about. To me, death is final. The end. But even so I have a phobia about being buried. When I die I'd rather they had me standing up, any way at all, but not buried.

It was a long trip to the Dolores cemetery. They drove that hearse like a taxicab, as fast as they could, with the mourners' bus following behind. Nothing like what I saw in California, where the hearse would proceed slowly as though with grief. Nobody in the bus cried on the way there. Some were even smiling as if they were on their way to a picnic.

When we arrived, Roberto and Consuelo got out to take care of the papers. A little later I saw them talking, and then they went over to the driver of the hearse who started up the motor and backed up to the little church opposite the office. I got out and joined them. Four men lowered the casket from the hearse, carried it into the church, and set it down on some benches. My sister spoke to the priest. It seems that before getting down to work, the holy man, out of Christian charity, said,

"That will be thirty *pesos*." Consuelo turned to me and made a face. "It's thirty *pesos*, brother." What could I do? I handed it over.

How few priests practice what they preach! I'm so steeped in business nowadays I can see clearly that the priests, too, are doing nothing but business. If some poor guy arrives, the priest pays no attention to him, but if one arrives in a nice automobile it's, "Yes, my son, here and, yes, my son, there." They buy him God's pardon and give him an automatic pass to Paradise. If you get married in church and you want a carpet, it'll cost you so much. If you want flowers, so much more. Singing? So much. There's a price list for everything, with a different charge for Purgatory, Heaven, and Paradise. What bastards!

After the Mass the undertaker came over to Roberto and said, "If you want us to take your relative as far as the canyon it will cost you another seventy-five *pesos*."

Buzzards, that's all they are . . . buzzards, I said to myself. I made up my mind not to give them another *centavo*. There was no money left anyway. When they saw that it was impossible to squeeze out any more, the men from the funeral parlor resigned themselves and took the body out of the church. They loaded it on the hearse again and we started off to my aunt's last resting place.

The pepper trees, the willows, and the other trees slid by as we rode through the cemetery. We passed the mausoleums of the wealthy and the less luxurious monuments of those not as rich. Here and there among them were some simple wooden crosses of the poor. Some graves had crucifixes inside a niche where candles were burning and flowers drooped, showing that the Day of the Dead was just over. There were some graves that were carefully tended, with pretty little gardens, begonias, lilies, *immortelles*, and an occasional rosebush.

We stopped at a section where there was an open grave almost at the foot of a big pepper tree. There were two big piles of brown earth, one at the head and the other at the foot of the grave. It seems they had removed someone else's remains out of the same grave. I saw leg bones still inside stockings and a skull that seemed to be smiling sarcastically at the other body about to go in. Getting out of the bus relieved our legs, and we all formed a semicircle, talking and looking around as if we were at the theatre. Our feet sank into the loose dirt which got into our shoes. They unloaded the casket and with some difficulty carried it to the grave.

It is hard to say what one feels at such moments, but I could swear that everybody had gooseflesh when the coffin was lowered to the edge of the grave. And then they began to act out the drama. "*Ayyy*, you are going, *comadrita*," somebody said, crying. "My *comadrita* is going . . ." "Gentlemen . . . anybody . . . let us see her once more for the last time . . . *Ayyy*, darling, you are going . . ." Ready to please, Roberto bent down, turned a screw that was like a handle, and opened the coffin. Several peered in to see the macabre sight . . . a few with hesitation, but all with curiosity.

Suddenly, everything, people, trees, plants, went blurred on account of the tears that came to my eyes. They closed the coffin, and the gravediggers put a length of webbing under it at each end and lowered it with difficulty into the pit. It barely fit. Even in her grave my aunt was hemmed in. When the casket touched bottom it was as if life stopped. Everybody stood motionless. Then Gaspar bent over and threw the first handful of earth into the hole. I saw many hands scoop up earth and do the same. I squatted, took my handful of dirt and tossed it onto the coffin. It made a disagreeable sound as it struck. I picked up a shovel, somebody else took another one, and we worked in turns until the grave was filled. It was as though we were in haste to bury memories as well as the body.

All that time, Roberto just stood there, clenching his fists, his eyes swimming in tears. Consuelo was shrieking rather than crying. Others were sobbing even though they had insulted or ignored my aunt when she was alive. I hate that kind of hypocrisy. It nauseates me. It's hard to explain the tears of a woman like *Señora* Catarina, who had shown such aversion toward my aunt. She had gossiped about her and even wanted to hit her, and yet there was Catarina crying her eyes out. She wasn't crying because she was sad but to keep in good with the relatives so that tomorrow or the next day she could ask a favor of them. I condemn tears like those.

Then there followed the little scene of placing the plants on the grave. Matilde said, "*Ay*, she was very fond of this fern. Put it there at the head."

"No, no, no, better at her feet," said Catarina.

While they were putting in the plants, Pancho broke a twig and looked around for some string to tie the pieces together to form a cross. Then Matilde said to Roberto and me, "Now you boys shouldn't neglect the grave if you want it to be nice. And let's see if we can come here next week to say a little prayer for her."

I thought to myself, "If I didn't treat her right when she was alive, now that she's dead . . ." It was the same with my mother and with my wife Paula.

Finally, we drove away through the canyon, thick with its beautiful, indifferent trees. "Good-bye . . . good-bye, Dolores cemetery. We go in grief leaving the last of the Vélezes in your entrails." Consuelo was the only one in the bus still crying as we left. She kept looking back through the rear window even when we were outside the cemetery.

"I still have to deal with her," I thought. I really couldn't stand my sister any more on account of her attitude toward me. Imagine, a few weeks ago she showed up at the market, screaming that I was a crook, that I hadn't paid her her money. If she had only said, "Brother, I'm broke. I need fifty *pesos*," I'd have answered, "Have things gone bad with you? Here, little sister." But she came at me with claws ready to scratch, so I wouldn't give her even five *centavos*.

I'm not like that with Roberto. When he's without a cent, I'm the first one he turns to and I give him ten, twenty, or fifty *pesos*. I bawl him out, of course, for drinking or for playing the big-shot with his friends, but I always help him. You see, when Roberto works with me in the market, I hold back some of his money—a hundred *pesos*, or two hundred—without his knowing it, but I do it so that when he comes to me for money I'll have some for him. The way I figure it, I clip him in order to help him save up something, and it works out fine.

But Consuelo is another matter. She doesn't trust me and never really gave me a chance to help her. She sees me as an enemy instead of as a brother. Why all that hatred against me? Why that phobia? Because when I was a kid I gave her a slap or two? If I had tried to commit a disgraceful act the way some brothers do to their sisters, she would have all the justification in the world. But I never did anything bad to her. Yes, I neglected my children now and then, but the responsibility for them was not on *her* shoulders. It didn't cost *her* anything. No, what she has against me is something sick, I cannot explain why.

What I'd like is to see her pride bent. I'd like her to fall so I could lift her up afterward, not because I want a total victory but to have her recognize that I am her elder brother and her superior. I'd like to see her in real misfortune so that she'll have to come to me for help. I swear I would do something for her then. If she were seriously ill, without hesitation I would pay whatever was needed to save her life. I've come to the realization that if I spend even a thousand *pesos* it's easy for me to replace them. I, who have never had anything, not even a spot to drop dead on, know now that the value of money in itself is very relative. So it wouldn't mean a thing for me to help my sister if she would only put aside her hatred of me.

What I am talking about, possibly, is the purchase of her love. But I have to be on guard with Consuelo because I am absolutely positive that if I try to get close to her she would throw my love back into my face with shit. I have enough of that with my wife from day to day and it has hurt me in a terrible way. I have to protect myself against that kind of suffering. That's why I can't make any move toward my sister, because the day I offer her my affection and she throws it back at me, I'll never be able to forgive her. We have not reached that extreme yet because up to now I haven't tried to come to an understanding with her. I've merely been indifferent. It's not that I don't feel love for her. It's a matter of fear.

When we got back to the *vecindad*, it was pretty late. María and I went to the restaurant where she worked and we had supper. My friends there invited me to a game of dominoes but I didn't want to play. I felt depressed, very depressed, and I went home early.

Roberto

THE priest never came to give my aunt the last rites. Gaspar had gone for him and he came back and told me, "The priest says he can't come because it's too far."

What a miserable priest, I said to myself. It's his duty to come. Besides, we were going to pay him, and even Christ himself didn't come to collect for his good deeds. I sent Gaspar to another priest, but he wouldn't come either, though he was only four blocks away. What a wicked mother that priest must have had, I thought. What are they for if not to aid the dying and the dead and help whoever is in need? I may not be a devout Catholic, but I do believe in God and His Commandments. I am not criticizing the Church, only those two priests for not coming when we called.

We waited and waited until finally the bus and the hearse arrived, with the crowd of curious children who

always run ahead of them. Everyone immediately piled
into the bus until it was full. Later we brought out my
aunt's coffin and I had to break the door frame a little
because it wasn't wide enough. My aunt was lifted onto
the hearse and I laid her flowers on top of the coffin.

When we had finished loading the hearse, the funeral
director asked me, "Who is in charge here?"

"I am, sir."

"Please pay me my money," he said.

"If you wish. It is customary to ask for payment at the
cemetery, but if you want it right now you can have it." I
still lacked thirty-five *pesos*, but Consuelo got them for
me and I paid him the four hundred *pesos*.

When we arrived at the Dolores cemetery, I asked the
driver to back up and let us off at the chapel. The priest
invited us to come in and then he asked us whether we
wanted a High Mass with music for thirty-five *pesos*, a
funeral Mass for twenty-five *pesos*, or a plain Mass for
fifteen *pesos*. I took it badly and told him, "I don't have
any money, and besides the services should all be the
same price." But I said to my brother and sister, "All
right, since my aunt hasn't been given the last rites why
should we haggle over the last few *centavos* we spend
on her?" I told the priest to go ahead and give us the
High Mass with music. And so he gave her the last rites,
the ashes, the holy water, the Extreme Unction, and I
don't know what else.

My brother was standing behind me and because of
that I couldn't pray or repeat what the priest said even
though I wanted to. It made me feel very bad. I don't
know what has happened to Manuel, but lately he has
denounced the priests and the saints very much. And
when he passes in front of a church, he spits and says,

"Bastards, they'll hear about it if they do anything to me." I've told him, "*Hombre*, brother, what's wrong with you? You can grab the hair of the devil if you want to, but you must respect the beliefs of others, don't you think? I don't approve of your saying things against the Church. Just leave them alone and don't talk like that." I'm worried about him, because I feel that he may be lost.

When the Mass was over, the priest said, "Now may we have an offering for us here?" By this time I was crying, because I felt the last moment had arrived for my aunt. I said, "Here, Father, I only have two *pesos* left, but take them."

"No, son, you keep them. Let the others give something if they want to."

We left and made our way to the spot below the ravine, where we buried my aunt. And so it ended.

We all returned to the house and Consuelo asked, "What shall we do now?"

"I don't know, sister. You have your own ideas of what to do with my aunt's things and with her house."

The day before, the landlord had come to collect the rent and some of the neighbors had taken him to one side to talk about getting my aunt's house. When he came over to us I said, "Good morning, sir. I want to tell you that my aunt died yesterday and it was her last wish that I should take charge of her house."

"Oh?" he said. "That may have been her last wish, but it isn't mine."

At that all the anger I had been holding back made me want to smash his face. He spoke so contemptuously and with such scorn that I had to back away from him to keep from hitting him. That is a great defect of mine. When I get angry I can't defend myself with words, only with my fists. So all I could say was, "Well then, what are you going to do?"

"Right now you have to bury the old lady," he said. "She was always good with me, so we can decide about the house later." And he left.

I was really boiling, and I thought, "What a shameless bastard he is to talk like that."

Meanwhile, Consuelo and Manuel were also fighting over what to do with the house and my aunt's belongings. Gaspar had sold his things to help pay for the funeral, and Consuelo wanted everything else to stay exactly as it was. She said to me, "Look, brother, it would be better if Gaspar stayed here. I've already told him that Matilde and Pancho are going to move in with him."

"I don't think it's a good idea because the landlord will raise the rent and they won't be able to pay it. Besides, they won't live peacefully together because they all drink. Right now Matilde and Pancho are not drinking because they have taken a vow, but as soon as the vow is over they're going to have a colossal binge to make up for it and then there's going to be a big battle. Gaspar has already said that if they move over he's going to throw out their furniture."

I knew it was not going to work out but I couldn't convince my sister. She said, "If my aunt had lived she would have wanted Gaspar to stay here, because she always stood up for him." And I had to agree. But before I went home, I took my mother's picture and a few of my favorite saints.

Consuelo

AT last the hearse and the funeral bus arrived. I felt my breast tighten. The hour of separation had come. When my aunt was carried out in my brothers' arms, I remembered her words, "I won't leave here until they carry me out feet first." How enormous a sadness I felt as I looked through the window of the hearse and saw her lying on her gray couch surrounded by flowers.

Matilde had brought alcohol and an onion in case I felt faint and Roberto stayed close to take care of me. His face, too, was wet with tears. Manuel glanced at me sideways, expecting me to give way to hysterical sobs, but I would not let him see me defeated. I carried myself proudly although my chest pained me and torment engulfed my throat.

We got into the bus and as we left I turned my face toward the *vecindad*. "Now, my little mother, you must leave forever. Here your house will stay. But don't worry, little one, I will take care of it." And so the funeral "procession" departed.

Unfortunately I had taken a seat behind Manuel and María and could hear their conversation. Manuel put his arm around his wife and they talked of business in the plaza. Not for a minute were their thoughts with us. Perhaps he was trying to distract me, because when we passed what had been the zone of the Nonoalco bridge he leaned forward and said to me, "The mayor has done some good here. As we go by take a look at the beautiful housing project he is putting up."

I scarcely turned my head to look, but rode along concentrating on my aunt, comforting and reassuring her. We passed by Avenida Melchor Campo, Avenida Gutenberg, Avenida Horacio where I once had friends and many illusions about my future. It was a world completely unknown to my aunt. She had never wanted to go out with me. All of them were a little afraid of me, because they say that I am severe and not like them. But I had loved her, and while we made that last trip I felt as if she were still watching over me, inviting me to go with her as she had when I was a child, turning her head to look for me, "And Skinny, where is she?"

"Here, dear one, I am here beside you." I felt that at any moment she would look around to see me. Scenes from her life passed through my mind.

I still hadn't seen her face, and I thought that when we arrived I would ask them to open the coffin. I had asked for holy water back at her house and someone had assured me that there would be water and a chapel where they could take the body and say a Mass. I had been looking forward to that. She should not go without some ceremony. So when we arrived we carried her coffin to the chapel where the priest, with a smile on his lips, invited us to enter. "Come in, come in. All who wish to may enter the house of God." But before giving the last rites he told us, "Thirty-five *pesos* for a Mass sung with the organ, twenty-five *pesos* for the ordinary Mass. You decide."

It offended me to see the disdainful way they commercialize and take advantage of these moments when grief keeps one from seeing clearly. Manuel, Roberto, Jaime, and I got together the money to pay for the Mass. I was glad to see Manuel make the move that most killed him, that is, to put his hand into his pocket and take out the money to pay his share.

The priest began to pray, and we knelt to join him. I bowed my head . . . the weight seemed so great that for a moment I thought I was going to fall, but Matilde held me by the shoulders. I raised my head and the faintness passed. My brother Roberto wept with bowed head. Matilde and Catarina did not cry; their daily lives are surrounded with grief and they have become immune. We sat down again, and I knew that the final moment was near. She would stay here, irrevocably alone. We would go back to resume our juggling on the tightrope of life.

The owner of the hearse charged us seventy-five *pesos*. It was more than we had agreed upon, but he said in this way he could give us a place that was not at the bottom of a gully. Manuel said that they take advantage of people at such times and I agreed. I was angry with my brother Roberto. My aunt had bought the right to a permanent plot in the cemetery and through his stupidity she was placed in another spot where she might be exhumed to make way for someone else. I continued to plead that she be buried with the rest of our family, but it wasn't possible.

At last I stood at the opening of the damp vault that was to receive her. I asked them to open the coffin. Manuel did not want to see her, but Roberto and I did. It comforted me to see her for the last time, her small face smooth yet with little furrows, wearing a faint expression of pain. Her eyes were beautiful, the lashes curled. I gazed on her with all my love, interring with her all the emotion that was within me. "Little mother . . . little mother . . ." I bit my lips.

They closed the coffin and began to lower it. I wanted to kiss it, but perhaps they thought I was going to throw myself in, because I felt hands holding me back.

As they finished filling the grave, I looked at the sky and at the surroundings. The place where she rested was lovely. She was at the foot of a large tree, like the *ahuehuete* tree she used to visit year after year on her pilgrimages to Chalma. There was greenery around her, and a little sun.

I asked God, Where do the poor find rest? Will they truly have rest? Tell me, oh God, what will happen after death to a life that has been lived in martyrdom? You have said, "Blessed are the poor, for theirs is the kingdom of heaven." But here they say, "We have to purify ourselves in the eternal fire." I rebel, oh Lord, not against Your holy purposes, but against what people say about the poor. I mourn Your life, oh Lord, told by a rosary of Your tears, by the blood of Your footsteps. But why, Lord, why this miserable death?

I knelt to smooth the earth over her as if I were

caressing her. One of my aunt's *comadres* found an
evergreen sprig and put it on the grave, "so she will live
forever." I arranged some flowers, her favorite ones, but
that devil of a wife of Manuel's moved them back and
mixed them with the rest. The horn began to honk
impatiently. I climbed into the coach, and when the
motor started something inside me was pulled apart.
Through the rear window of the bus I could see her
grave. She was alone and there she had to stay.

We came back. I fled to the emptiness of her room.
Roberto left, saying that he was tired. Manuel went back
to the Casa Grande with María, saying, "In any case
I am going to get something out of this. Think about it
and we'll see." Matilde and Catarina returned to their
little home. I stayed in my aunt's kitchen. Gaspar went
into the bedroom and began to sob. Chocolate, the dog,
scrambled to his feet. I wondered what would become of
the dog and of my aunt's pigeons and cat. She and my
uncle had always been fond of all their pets but Chocolate
was their favorite. My aunt had treated him like her
child and really, that dog did understand a lot. She would
say to him, "Chocolate, come on in! You bark a lot, but
when it gets right down to it you come around to lick
my hand. You're all repentance, like that son of a bitch
shrimp of a master of yours." And she would pick up her
sandal and threaten him. When finally Chocolate came
in and jumped into his box, she'd say, "Coward! You
barked as if you meant business."

How I felt my aunt's absence! Gaspar came into the
kitchen and after a while we began to talk. "Excuse me,
Señorita Consuelo, what your brother said, that he would
give me permission to stay here for only a few days . . .

well, after all, it's for you to say, isn't it? It's no less than I could hope for."

"No, Gaspar, he has no right to tell you to go. Roberto did not know how to explain it well. You stay in the house. Matilde wants it too, but don't be upset. Tomorrow we'll see how to arrange things."

"Yes, but look, she has already started to take out some things. She took the glasses that were over there."

"Don't worry, Gaspar. She'll bring them back. And the brazier?"

"She took that too."

"I'll tell her to bring it back."

We spoke of my aunt, of the disputes they had had. He swore again and again that the stories were not true. I listened indifferently.

Matilde came over to invite me to eat with them. As we entered the house, her father, José, arrived and shouted, "What happened? What do you want me for?"

I realized that they wanted to talk about my aunt's place. Well, at least they had shown a little tact in inviting me to sit down at their table. At any other time I would have refused, but this time I forgot my repugnance at eating there. I even forgot the odor from the toilets that Catarina never cleaned. I sat on the bed next to Señor José. To my left, on a board placed over a pail, Pancho sat with Matilde's young son beside him. Her daughter sat on the floor. Pancho turned a large pot upside down and used it as a table. Matilde was in the kitchen with her grandmother; Catarina served the food. They had prepared stewed chicken, the best food they had, for this day. They gave me hot chicken soup, bless them. It was something out of the ordinary in their lives. While she was serving, Catarina put bits of *taco* in her mouth and made jokes, trying to get me to forget. What affection I felt for them at that moment! The way in which one expresses concern for others may be insignificant, but the results are great.

Before they brought up the subject, I asked them, "It's about the house, isn't it? I understand that Matilde needs it. We don't have to decide right now, do we? There's plenty of time, and I'm so tired. Let's wait until tomorrow so we can go to our villas to rest and sun ourselves. We'll take a vacation first!" I made a sweeping gesture that made them all laugh.

The soup tasted delicious and the sauce that Matilde had made was also very good. I told her so and she replied like a child who has received a compliment, "Ay, yes . . . Ay, no, it's very poor." I told her that it didn't taste just right because Gaspar hadn't eaten yet and I asked them to call him. He didn't want to come until I sent word that "I, *Señorita* Consuelo, say you are to come or I will go after you."

"Oh," said Catarina, "Roberto told him that he wasn't to touch a drop of wine."

"Yes, but I told Roberto that life is sacred, and we have no right to interfere in Gaspar's."

"But if he drinks he might become indecent, as he did at the wake," said Matilde.

"Look, don't pay any attention to him. Just let him talk," I told her. "This happens to everyone when they drink. The same thing has happened to you, yes, even to my aunt when they were passing the bottle around."

Gaspar came in. "You sent for me, *Señorita* Consuelo?"

"Sit down, Gaspar, and have something to eat."

"Maybe he doesn't want to," said Catarina. "I've invited him many times before and he didn't come."

When the meal was over I asked Matilde to return the brazier and the glasses and told Catarina to look after the house. I implored them to recite a rosary and then to eat docilely.

"But now you want to, don't you, Gaspar?" He began I said good-bye, leaving by the path in the courtyard where I had so often come in search of peace or comfort for my soul.

I went to spend the night at my half-sister Antonia's house. On my last trip to Mexico City I had brought from the north some new clothing that I wanted to sell. I left some dresses with Antonia and promised to give her a commission if she sold them. I did the same with my sister Marta but she took the clothing back to Acapulco with her and I hadn't heard from her since. I hoped that Antonia had some money for me. I needed it so badly!

Antonia and her husband were surprised to see me. "Why didn't you let us know you were coming?"

"There wasn't time. I have just come from my aunt's funeral."

"And why didn't anyone let us know?"

"I don't know. I just arrived this morning."

They were playing popular music on the record player, with the volume turned up high. Antonia wore a new gold dressing gown which surprised me because fifteen days before she didn't have enough money to buy a comb and I had left her mine. We had a drink and then my brother-in-law left to go after a dress he had bought his daughter for her birthday party the next day. With some misgivings, I asked Antonia about the money for the clothes. "What happened, Tonia? Did you sell the things?"

"Yes, Consuelo, but can you believe it? They haven't paid me yet."

I didn't say anything but I knew what had happened. She had bought clothes for herself and her daughter and only God knew if I would ever get my money. I kept silent and asked her little girl to join me in saying a rosary before we went to bed. "You'd better hurry and say your prayers before my husband gets back," Antonia said. "You know he doesn't like these things." We were still praying when he came in, but he respected our feelings and didn't protest.

The following day, with the little money I had left, I paid my aunt's landlord part of the four months' rent she owed him. He agreed to wait for the rest. Then I went back to the *vecindad* and at last convinced Gaspar and Matilde to share my aunt's place. I told Matilde she could move in on condition that she would take care of everything as if my aunt were still there. To honor her memory, the altar and the religious pictures especially were to remain as they were. Whether they meant it or not, Matilde and Gaspar agreed. Then I went through my aunt's possessions, and divided them up between the two of them and a few friendly neighbors. For myself I kept the shawl I had sent my aunt money for. It was her pride, Gaspar told me. I also took her papers, her scissors, and two figures of the *Niño Dios*, and I got back the iron she had pawned. I didn't want to see anyone else use the clothes she wore the most, so I burned them. Then I gave some money to the woman who had helped her, five *pesos* to Gaspar, one to Matilde for her child's milk, and one to my godchild. I gave them my address and left, promising to return. It was late and again I slept at Antonia's.

The next morning I bought my return ticket to Nuevo Laredo and went to Manuel's house to get his signature giving permission for his children to leave the country. He was eating breakfast. Roberto was sitting on a bench outside waiting for him. By lying a little, I had no trouble getting Manuel to sign the papers. He didn't care enough about the children to even ask any questions. Before I left, I gave Roberto ten *pesos*.

All that day I walked alone. In the afternoon I looked for a church, went into a *café*, and finally left on the bus, carrying with me more grief and sorrow than I had ever borne before, my body in tatters and my whole life a moan.

Appendix

ᓚᓰ$\mathbf{M}$ost (60.8 percent) of the money in the *vecindad* was invested in furniture and clothing; furniture accounted for one-third of the expenditures and clothing for one-fourth. The majority of items were bought new but 34.8 percent of the furniture and 12.7 percent of the clothing were bought second-hand. As one would expect, the poorer families bought most of the used articles. If we compare the three poorest families, which include Guadalupe, with the three richest families, we find an inverse ratio, that is, the poorest families bought 78 percent of their possessions second-hand whereas the richest families bought 76 percent of their possessions new.

Of the total value of possessions, 87 percent was acquired by cash purchases by the families themselves, 10.8 percent were received as gifts, and 2.2 percent were manufactured at home. In the case of Guadalupe, however, more than half (55.1 percent) of what she owned had been given to her. The gifts she received were valued at $66.77 whereas her purchases amounted to $54.16. Over 84 percent of her clothing, 59 percent of her religious objects, 34 percent of her household goods, 33 percent of her bedclothes, and 30 percent of her furniture were gifts. She ranked lowest in the *vecindad* in cash expenditures. Nothing that she owned was made at home.

Guadalupe ranked low in almost every category of possession—lowest in clothing, next to lowest in personal adornments and bed clothing, third lowest in furniture, fifth lowest in household equipment and decorative objects, and sixth lowest in kitchen utensils. She ranked first, however, in number and value of religious objects. She had twenty-three religious pictures and other objects with a total value of $35.12. Of these, almost 60 percent were gifts.

Most of the buying in shops and markets occurred within a one-mile radius of the *vecindad*. Of the new furniture, 63.7 percent was bought in the local public markets. A good deal of exchange, particularly of used goods, took place within the *vecindad* itself and among friends and relatives in the neighborhood. Almost 70 percent of the used furniture was acquired in this way.

Of the furniture, at least one of the following five articles were found in every dwelling unit: a bed, a mattress, a table, a set of shelves for dishes, and a shelf for an altar. These furnishings were considered essential for a minimum standard of living although most of the residents had lived without some or all of them in the past.

Beds and mattresses were the most costly items and somewhat of a status symbol. They took up most of the space in the small rooms and were used for many purposes—as chairs, worktables, play areas for children, and for sorting laundry. Men with night jobs slept during the day while members of the family sat, worked, played, or ate on the other side of the bed.

Despite their desirability, there were only twenty-three beds for the eighty-four people in the *vecindad*. Many still slept on straw *petates* or pieces of cardboard on the floor. Nine families each had two beds, usually one a double bed, the other a narrow cot because of lack of space. Two of the families had no mattress for their second bed and slept on newspapers and a thin cotton blanket spread over the springs.

Five families bought their beds new, the rest of the beds were bought second-hand, either in the Tepito market or from personal acquaintances. The most expensive new bed in the *vecindad* cost $12.00. The used beds ranged in cost from $2.80 to $8.00. Three beds were received as gifts. Although residence in the *vecindad* was quite stable and beds did not quickly wear out, the average time of possession of the beds was only four years, eight months. The rapid turnover of beds reflected the continual changes that occurred in the crowded little dwellings—births, deaths, marriages, shifting occupants, illness, drunkenness, or other family crises, which often required selling, pawning, or giving away furniture.

Mattresses posed a problem for many of the families. Because of their poor quality, the hard wear to which they were exposed, and the lack of protection given them, mattresses had to be replaced rather frequently. The average time of possession was three years, eight months. After that time, they were usually too lumpy, stained, torn, or infested with vermin to be used and had to be thrown out, burned, or given to less fastidious persons. Few *vecindad* mattresses had resale value although some used ones were purchased outside the *vecindad*. More mattresses than beds were bought new, at prices ranging from $2.80 to $7.50. Three families had bought expensive innerspring mattresses on credit at inflated prices ranging from $22.40 to $44.00. No down payment was required on credit buying but prices were almost doubled.

Other indispensable furnishings found in the fourteen dwellings were twenty-four tables, twenty dish-shelves or closets, and fourteen altars. Chairs were also very desirable articles of furniture; only one home was without any chair at all. There was a total of fifty-two chairs in the fourteen dwellings, greatly adding to the crowding.

In the absence of closets, wardrobes were needed for storage. Every home but two had a wardrobe of some kind. All the families had had a radio for some period in their lives. At the time of our study, three families had lost their radios through pawning, failure to meet credit payments, or inability to have them repaired. There were two TV sets in the *vecindad* at the time of our study, but one was soon lost by pawning. A third set had been lost a few years earlier and the same man, Guillermo Gutiérrez, bought another on credit, committing himself to paying $24.00 a month for it, with little likelihood that he would be able to do so.

Other furnishings found in the fourteen dwellings included three sewing machines, sixteen electric irons, two ironing boards, seven clocks, one electric heater, one step ladder, twelve scissors, fourteen kerosene stoves and four charcoal braziers. Because most of the dwellings had dirt floors, there were sixteen brooms but no mops, and because of the absence of water in the homes, there was a great abundance of pitchers, pails, and wash tubs. Most families had the basic cooking and serving utensils but there were only five garbage cans, five trays, four salt-cellars, two sugar bowls, and two ashtrays. There were only three toothbrushes in the *vecindad*. On the other hand, there were 147 pictures of Catholic saints, an average of over ten per room. These pictures had a total value of $210.52.

Clothing ranked second in the total outlay for material goods. It represented 27.4 percent of all purchases and ranked first in articles manufactured at home. Generally, a family that invested heavily in clothing tended to spend little on furniture and vice versa. Eighty percent of all the clothing was bought new. The middle-income families bought most of the second-hand clothing and, surprisingly, it was the better-off families that received more gifts of clothing. Guadalupe and Ignacio, the poorest family, was an exception in that most of their clothing had been given to them. Of the forty-three pieces of clothing they owned, they had purchased only one themselves.

For the twenty adult women in the *vecindad* there was a total of seventy-five dresses, an average of less than four apiece. Girls fourteen and under owned an average of six dresses apiece. All of the women had one pair of shoes; some of the children had more than one. In general, the young daughters had more clothing than their mothers. They wore brassieres, underpants, slips, sweaters, and coats when often their mothers did not. Of the fifteen pairs of stockings in the *vecindad*, most belonged to teen-age girls. Of the four people who had handkerchiefs, two were girls and two were men. Of the seven ladies' coats, five belonged to daughters. Older women wore the Mexican *rebozo* or sweaters. The only pocketbook in the *vecindad* was owned by a young lady. The one bathrobe in the *vecindad* was owned by a young married woman.

The men all owned shoes, a pair of pants, a shirt, and underpants and either a jacket or sweater to protect them from the cold. Two men owned a coat. Three men owned no socks, four had no undershirt, and no men owned a tie or a suit. The two suits in the *vecindad* were bought as boy's confirmation suits. One person, a man, owned a bathing suit.

Tools and equipment, owned mostly by the artisans who worked at home, ranked next in value and represented 7.9 percent of the total purchases. Bedclothing accounted for 6.8 percent. Every household had one or more sheets, pillows, and blankets or quilts. The latter were comparatively expensive items costing anywhere from $3.20 to $16.00 and were sometimes bought on the installment plan. Some of the bedclothing was made at home, especially by the poorer families. Of the seventy homemade articles, thirty-eight were sheets made of *manta*, a cheap cotton, often obtained from flour sacks.

Jewelry and wrist watches amounted to 3.1 percent of the value of all items purchased. Four families, all in the upper-income category, owned five wrist watches. Six religious medals and one silver crucifix, also found among the upper-income category, were valued at $30.56. There were twenty-five rings distributed among nine families and twenty pairs of earrings among eight families. There were no necklaces, bracelets, or brooches. As jewelry is easily pawned, the average length of possession of such articles was only 9.8 months. Seven families had forty-one toys, including a bicycle that was rented out. The toys represented 3 percent of all purchases.

OSCAR LEWIS was born in New York City in 1914 and grew up on a small farm in upstate New York. He received his Ph.D. in anthropology from Columbia University in 1940; he taught at Brooklyn College and Washington University and has been a professor of anthropology at the University of Illinois since 1948. He has also been the recipient of various distinguished fellowships and grants.

From his first visit to Mexico in 1943, Mexican peasants and city dwellers have been among his major interests. His book *Life in a Mexican Village: Tepoztlán Restudied* initiated a whole new trend in independent restudies in anthropology. In addition to *A Death in the Sánchez Family,* his other studies of Mexican life include *Five Families, Pedro Martínez* and *The Children of Sánchez.* He is also the author of *La Vida: A Puerto Rican Family in the Culture of Poverty—San Juan and New York,* which received the National Book Award. A further study of Puerto Rican culture, *Six Women,* will be published in 1971. *Anthropological Essays,* a collection of twenty-four essays, written over a period of twenty-five years, was published in 1970.

Professor Lewis is now in Cuba on a research program to study family and community life.

VINTAGE WORKS OF SCIENCE
AND PSYCHOLOGY